THE WOMAN'S PRAYER COMPANION

DEDICATION

*For the married, single, and professed religious women in the
Association of Contemplative Sisters
whose fidelity to prayer was the inspiration for this book.*

HOW TO USE THIS BOOK

This *Woman's Prayer Companion* consists of Life Events and Women of Inspiration and sets of suggested Psalms to use with any chosen selection. A **Psalm** follows each of the given antiphons. The **Antiphon** is generally prayed before and after the psalm. Three Psalms are used for each office. If two or more people are praying together, the verses of the psalms are alternated; i.e., one person or set of persons prays a verse, then another person or set of persons prays the following verse.

After the praying of the psalms, a suggested **Reflection** is given for silent meditation or faith sharing among those praying together. Other readings may be substituted. The **Responsory** is begun by the leader and the group repeats the prayer as indicated by the parts printed in bold print.

After the antiphon for the **Canticle** is prayed, one may use the Canticle of Zechariah (on the last page) or the Canticle of Mary (on the inside back cover). Traditionally the Canticle of Zechariah is prayed in the morning and the Canticle of Mary is prayed in the evening. But the office chosen may dictate the preference of the group.

The **Intercessions** are begun by the leader and the group prays the response together. It is suggested that those praying add their own petitions after reading the intercessions given.

The **Prayer** can be prayed by the leader or all together.

i

CONTENTS
Life Events

Contents

Psalms

Women of Inspiration

January

Contents

The women appearing in this book
are but a sampling of the many heroic
women of inspiration that could be included.
Each of you knows others that have
shaped and influenced history.
We hope that this book will encourage
you to celebrate the women
who have been a source of inspiration to you.

LIFE EVENTS

AGING

MORNING/EVENING PRAYER

(Psalms for the Aging, p. 57)

Ant 1 How attractive is wisdom in the aged, and understanding and counsel.

Ant 2 Rich experience is the crown of the elderly, and their boast is love of the Most High.

Ant 3 She will be fed with the bread of understanding and given the water of wisdom to drink.

REFLECTION/SHARING

...Alas, the springtime of my life is gone. From this old stump, watered by the grace of the Blood shed on Calvary, may there shoot forth sprouts like from those big trees in Virginia which were cut down, like my past life. Behold, the ground beneath them brings forth little green branches, which in time will become trees.

Blessed Katharine Drexel

RESPONSORY

They still bring forth fruit in old age; they are ever full of sap and green. **—They still...**
To show that God is upright; **—they are...**
Glory to you, Source of all Being, Eternal Word and Holy Spirit.
—They still...

CANTICLE

Ant When I see this "living light" all sadness and anxiety are taken away from me. The result is that I feel like a simple young girl and not like an old lady. (Hildegard of Bingen)

INTERCESSIONS:

O God, when we experience limitation in our physical abilities;
—increase our inner vitality and give us a youthful spirit.

When tiredness and fatigue overcome us;
   —mellow our tendency to be short-tempered and enable us
   to respond to others graciously.
As we grow more comfortable with the familiar;
   —give us a spirit of adventure and keep us open to the
   new and creative.
When we encounter immaturity in the young;
   —give us patience and wisdom in sharing our experience.
As each year passes;
   —fill our hearts with gratitude for the journey that has
   gone before and the journey yet to come.

PRAYER: O God, we thank you for the gift of years; for the opportunity to see the pattern of our lives and to have experienced the deaths from which we have risen over and over again. As we continue our journey, give us lightness of step and lightness of heart that we may grace our world with a spirit of joy and gratitude. We ask this in the name of Jesus who has gone before and continues to walk the way with us. Amen.

ANONYMOUS WOMEN

MORNING/EVENING PRAYER

(Psalms for Social Justice, p. 82; Times of Distress, p. 67)

Ant 1 How long, O God? Will you forget me forever?

Ant 2 You know my reproach and my shame and my dishonor; my foes are all known to you.

Ant 3 Let not the flood sweep over me, or the deep swallow me up, or the pit close its mouth over me.

REFLECTION/SHARING

For Zion's sake I will not keep silent,
and for Jerusalem's sake I will not rest,
until her vindication goes forth as brightness,
and her salvation as a burning torch. (Is: 62:1–4)

RESPONSORY

Keep me as the apple of your eye; hide me in the shadow of your
wings; **—Keep me...**
From the wicked who despoil me, **—hide me...**
Glory to you, Source of all Being, Eternal Word and Holy Spirit.
—Keep me...

CANTICLE

Ant Guard my life and deliver me, O God; let me not be put
to shame, for I take refuge in you.

INTERCESSIONS:

Jesus, one who served you, we know only as Peter's mother-in-
law;
——bless all nameless women who so generously serve others
and let them know their worth.
Peter's wife and the wives of the apostles are never mentioned;
——may women who have been so invisible in recorded history
find their rightful place as equal shapers of the destiny of
this universe.
Thousands of innocent nameless women were accused of
witchcraft and were tortured and killed by ecclesiastical and
civil authorities;
——enable us to forgive the many wrongs that have been
inflicted on women even as we strive for justice.
In many countries, women's only value is to produce male
offspring;
——may all women be recognized as children of God with
inherent self-worth.
Young girls are often denied the right to an education, the
right to serve at liturgy, the right to determine their own
destiny;
——give our daughters wise counselors and role models that
they may claim their inheritance as children of God in this
world.

PRAYER: O God, you created us in your image, both male
and female, yet women and their children are not

recognized as such. They are denied their rights in the church and in society. We cry out to you as Esther cried out for her people, to be with us and give us the courage to claim our birthright as your children. We ask this of you, our Mother/Father God in whose image we are. Amen.

AT TIMES OF ABANDONMENT

MORNING/EVENING PRAYER

(Psalms in Times of Distress, p. 67 or p. 69)

Ant 1 I am sure that neither death, nor life, nor angels nor principalities, nor things present, nor things to come, nor powers, nor height, nor depth, nor anything else in all creation, will be able to separate me from the love of God in Christ Jesus our Lord.

Ant 2 The Spirit helps us in our weakness, for we do not know how to pray as we ought, but the Spirit intercedes for us with sighs too deep for words.

Ant 3 Peace I leave with you; my peace I give to you; not as the world gives do I give to you. Let not your hearts be troubled, neither let them be afraid.

REFLECTION/SHARING

My God, my God, why have you forsaken me?
Why are you so far from helping me, from the words of my
   groaning?
O my God, I cry by day, but you do not answer;
   and by night, but find no rest.
Yet you are holy, enthroned on the praises of Israel.
In you our ancestors trusted;
   they trusted, and you did deliver them.
Be not far from me, for trouble is near,
   and there is no one to help.

Psalm 22:1–5

RESPONSORY

I will not leave you desolate; I will come to you. —**I will**...
Yet a little while; —**I will**...
Glory to you, Source of all Being, Eternal Word and Holy Spirit.
   —**I will**...

CANTICLE

Ant As a hart longs for flowing streams, so longs my soul
      for you, O God.

INTERCESSIONS:

Hagar was sent out into the wilderness with her son Ishmael;
   —O God, give all who feel abandoned the assurance of your
      steadfast care.
The daughter of Jephthah was given over to her death;
   —grant that all women have the right to determine their
      own destiny.
Susanna was falsely accused and no one but a stranger came
to her defense;
   —comfort all who feel themselves forsaken by family or
      friends.
Jesus, you felt abandoned by your friends in the Garden and
forsaken by God on the cross;
   —at times of desolation give us the courage to persevere
      until the darkness passes.
You were betrayed by one you had chosen—one who sat with
you at table;
   —heal the wounds inflicted by those we have loved, and give
      us the grace to forgive.
Your Mother's heart was wounded with sorrow as she lost you
to the cross;
   —be consolation and hope for all who journey with the
      dying.

PRAYER: Jesus, you felt the darkness of the tomb, in faith
          waiting the dawn of the resurrection that was yet
          to come. When we feel so alone give us the
          assurance we need, that we too will some day

experience your resurrection in us. We long for
your peace and the joy we once knew. Come,
Lord Jesus, come! Amen.

BATTERED AND ABUSED

MORNING/EVENING PRAYER

(Psalms for Social Justice, p. 82; Times of Distress, p. 67)

Ant 1 "Hail, King of the Jews!" And they spat upon him and
took the reed and struck him on the head.

Ant 2 For the mountains may depart and the hills be
removed, but my steadfast love shall not depart from
you.

Ant 3 Violence shall no more be heard in your land,
devastation or destruction within your borders, for
our God will be your everlasting light.

REFLECTION/SHARING

When you pass through the waters I will be with you;
and through the rivers, they shall not overwhelm you;
when you walk through fire you shall not be burned,
and the flame shall not consume you.
Because you are precious in my eyes,
and honored, and I love you. (Is 43:2, 3–4)

RESPONSORY

No more shall you be called Forsaken, but you shall be
called My Delight. —**No more**...
Your land shall no more be termed Desolate; —**but you**...
Glory to you, Source of all Being, Eternal Word and Holy Spirit.
—**No more**...

CANTICLE

Ant For behold I create new heavens and a new earth; and
the former things shall not be remembered or come into
mind.

INTERCESSIONS:

Lot offered his daughters to a hostile crowd to be raped;
—protect women who find themselves defenseless in oppressive situations; women who are victims of war and violence.

Jephthah sacrificed his only daughter to fulfill a vow;
—protect children who are victims of cults and misguided beliefs.

Tamar, the daughter of David, was raped by her half-brother;
—heal the wounds of children who have been violated by those they trusted.

To protect his male guests, the virgin daughter of an Ephraimite was given to a crowd to be abused;
—hear the cries of women who are battered and abused in their own homes.

Susanna was falsely accused of infidelity and condemned to death;
—may women's voices be heard and believed so that justice may serve them.

PRAYER: O God, down through the ages you have seen the battered bodies of women and children. With the broken body of Jesus hanging on the cross, they carry the burden of sin and violence in a world you created out of love. Give each of us the grace to unburden our hearts of hate and retaliation so that we may transform this suffering into redemptive love. Heal the hearts that wound and the bodies that are wounded so that we may know both as your sons and daughters, and each as sisters and brothers. We ask this through our brother, Jesus, whose wounds have brought salvation to all. Amen.

BIRTH OR ADOPTION OF A CHILD

MORNING/EVENING PRAYER

(Psalms for Mothers, p. 81; Feasts, p. 75)

Ant 1 When a woman is in travail she has sorrow because her hour has come; but when she is delivered of the child, she no longer remembers the anguish, for joy that a child is born into the world.

Ant 2 Simeon took the Child in his arms and blessed God and said, "Lord, now let your servant depart in peace, for my eyes have seen your salvation."

Ant 3 Jesus said, "Let the children come to me, and do not hinder them; for to such belongs the realm of heaven."

REFLECTION/SHARING

The disciples came to Jesus, saying, "Who is the greatest in the realm of heaven?" And calling to him a child, he put the child in the midst of them and said, "Truly, I say to you, unless you turn and become like children, you will never enter the realm of heaven." (Mt 18:1–5)

RESPONSORY

Blessed is the one who fears God; your children will be like olive plants around your table. —**Blessed**...
May you see your children's children; —**like olive**...
Glory to you, Source of all Being, Eternal Word and Holy Spirit. —**Blessed**...

CANTICLE

Ant Grandchildren are the crown of the aged, and children the glory of their parents.

INTERCESSIONS:

O God, you have visited the earth and greatly enriched it;
—we give you thanks for the gift of this child which you have given to grace our earth.

With longing and expectation Mary and Joseph awaited the
coming of Jesus, Emmanuel, God with us;
  —may our joy in the presence of this new child among us
    surround it with love and security.
You, O God, are both Mother and Father to us: our wholly
Available One;
  —grant that all who welcome this child into this family be
    nurturers both of its bodily needs and its life in the Spirit.
You placed Jesus in the care of Mary and Joseph;
  —bless those responsible for the care of this child: give them
    the means to support it and the wisdom to guide it.
As we marvel in the gift of the child you have given us;
  —we pray that it may live in a world where there is peace
    and justice for all.

PRAYER: O God, the presence of a child among us fills us
        with joy and awe. Help us to make our world a
        welcoming place for all children—free from fear of
        war, hunger, violence, and all forms of abuse.
        May this child know you through those of us who
        love it, and may it grow in wisdom, age, and
        grace all the days of its life. We ask this in the
        name of Jesus who invited all children to come to
        him. Amen.

CARING FOR AN ELDERLY PARENT

MORNING/EVENING PRAYER

(Psalms for the Aging, p. 57; Every Day, p. 71)

Ant 1 Kindness to parents will not be forgotten; in the day
        of your affliction, it will be remembered in your favor.

Ant 2 O God, you are the companion of all who fear you, of
        those who keep your precepts.

Ant 3 Teach me good judgment and knowledge, for I believe
        in your commandments.

REFLECTION/SHARING

Ruth bore a son. Then the women said to Naomi, "Blessed be God, who has not left you this day without next of kin. He shall be to you a restorer of life and a nourisher of your old age; for your daughter-in-law who loves you, who is more to you than seven sons, has borne him." (Ruth 4:14–15)

RESPONSORY

Those who wait for God shall renew their strength; they shall run and not be weary. —**Those who**...
They shall walk and not faint; —**they shall run**...
Glory to you, Source of all Being, Eternal Word and Holy Spirit. —**Those**...

CANTICLE

Ant Blessed are the merciful, for they shall obtain mercy.

INTERCESSIONS:

O God, we have been nurtured and guided both by you and by our parents;
    —when we become the caregivers for our parents, enable us to be nurturing and compassionate.
When our time and mobility is limited because of our responsibility to care for our elderly parents;
    —help us to remember our early years when they gave of their time and sustenance.
As they see themselves becoming helpless and dependent;
    —grant that we may care for them in ways that preserve their dignity and sense of self.
If the time should come that we can no longer care for them and difficult decisions must be made;
    —give us peace of mind and trust in your loving providence.
As we care for the elderly, help us to realize we are preparing for our own aging process;
    —knowing that our dying years are years of pregnancy awaiting birth to eternal life.

PRAYER: O God, we give you thanks for our parents and for the gift of being able to serve them. Give us patience and compassion in difficult times, and gratitude for times of joy and celebration. May we realize the gift of preparing our parents for the life that is yet to come, when they will be freed from all that binds and limits them. We ask this in the name of Jesus that he may companion them along the way. Amen.

CHANGE OF CAREER

MORNING/EVENING PRAYER

(Psalms for Every Day, p. 71 or p. 73)

Ant 1 And Mary said to the angel, "How shall this be, since I have no husband?" And the angel said to her, "The Holy Spirit will come upon you, and the power of the Most High will overshadow you."

Ant 2 The angel said to Mary, "And behold, your kinswoman Elizabeth in her old age has also conceived a son; and this is the sixth month with her who was called barren. For with God, nothing will be impossible."

Ant 3 Jesus said to Simon, "Do not be afraid; henceforth you will be catching people." And when they had brought their boats to land, they left everything and followed him.

REFLECTION/SHARING

May you, O God, grant that I speak with judgment and have thoughts worthy of what I have received,
for you are the guide even of wisdom and the corrector of the wise.
For both we and our words are in your hand, as are all understanding and skill in crafts.

For it is you who gave me unerring knowledge of what exists,
to know the structure of the world and the activity of the
    elements;
the beginning and the end and middle of times,
the alterations of the solstices and the changes of the
    seasons,
the cycles of the year and the constellations of the stars.
(Wis 7:15–19)

RESPONSORY

Unless you are born of water and the Spirit, you cannot enter
    the realm of God; —**Unless**...
You must be born anew; — **or you cannot**...
Glory to you, Source of all Being, Eternal Word and Holy Spirit.
    —**Unless**...

CANTICLE

Ant Ananias, laying hands on him, said to Saul, "The Lord
    Jesus, who appeared to you on the road by which you
    came, has sent me that you may regain sight and be
    filled with the Holy Spirit."

INTERCESSIONS:

Although he was well-established Abraham was called forth to
a new land;
    —keep us open to the voices and circumstances that lead
    us in new directions.
Paul, a tentmaker called to be an apostle, found difficulty in
being accepted as such;
    —help us to withstand obstacles and misunderstanding
    as we venture into new territory.
Elizabeth Seton, a mother of five and a widow, founded a
religious congregation at the age of thirty-five; Grandma Moses
became a painter at the age of seventy-six;
    —make us aware of your Creative Spirit ever working
    within us.
The angel commissioned the women at the tomb, to go forth
and proclaim to the disciples that Jesus had risen;

—give us patience with ourselves in our new beginnings and enable us to trust the gifts and talents you have given us. Forced to give up teaching, Edith Stein trusted in providence and eventually followed her call to religious life;
—when our careers are forcibly terminated, give us the courage to believe in your loving and provident care.

PRAYER: O God, your ways are not our ways—and your thoughts are not our thoughts. Give us the grace to trust you when the direction of our lives is changed by circumstances or by call. Help us to realize that you are God-Weaver, and our lives a tapestry ever new and unfolding. As we reach life's end may it be your work—pleasing to you and a gift to humanity. We ask this in the name of Jesus who is our way, our truth, and our life. Amen.

CONFIRMATION OF A YOUNG WOMAN
(For Dana)

MORNING/EVENING PRAYER

Ant 1 O God, you are a light to my eyes, a lamp for my feet.

Psalm 119:9–16

How shall the young
  remain sinless?
By living according to your
  word.
I have sought you with all
  my heart;
let me not stray from your
  commands.

I carry your word in my
  heart
lest I sin against you.
Blessed are you, O God;
teach me your statutes.

With my lips I have
  recounted
all the decrees of your
  mouth.
I delight to do your will
as though all riches were
  mine.

I will meditate on your
  precepts
and fix my eyes on your
  ways.—

I will delight in your
statutes;
I will not forget your word.

Glory to you Source of all
Being, Eternal Word and
Holy Spirit.

As it was in the beginning,
is now and will be
forever. Amen.

**Ant 2 We are your
people, chosen before
the foundation of the
world.**

Ephesians 1:3–10

Praised be the God
of our Lord Jesus Christ,
who has blessed us in
Christ
with every spiritual
blessing in the heavens.

God chose us in him
before the foundation of
the world,
that we should be holy
and blameless in God's
sight.

We have been predestined
to be God's children
through Jesus Christ;
such was the purpose of
God's will,
that all might praise the
glorious favor
bestowed on us in Christ.

In Christ and through his
blood,
we have redemption,
the forgiveness of our sins,
according to the riches of
God's grace lavished
upon us.

For God has made known
to us,
in all wisdom and insight,
the mystery of the plan set
forth in Christ.

A plan to be carried out in
Christ,
in the fullness of time,
to unite all things in
Christ,
things in heaven and
things on earth.

Glory to you Source of all
Being, Eternal Word and
Holy Spirit.

As it was in the beginning,
is now and will be
forever. Amen.

**Ant 3 Jesus was revealed
in the breaking of the
bread, alleluia.**

Revelation 19:1,5–7

Salvation, glory, and power
belong to you;
your judgments are honest
and true.

All of us, your servants,
sing praise to you;—

we worship you reverently,
both great and small.

You, our almighty God, are
Creator of heaven and
earth.
Let us rejoice and exult,
and give you glory.

The wedding feast of the
Lamb has begun,—

and the bride has made
herself ready.

Glory to you Source of all
Being, Eternal Word and
Holy Spirit.

As it was in the beginning,
is now and will be
forever. Amen.

REFLECTION/SHARING

Youth may be headstrong, but it will advance its allotted
length. Through the ages in the battle with the powers of
evil—with poverty, misery, ignorance, war, ugliness, and
slavery—youth has steadily turned on the enemy. That is
why I never turn away from the new generation impatiently
because of its knowingness. Through it alone shall salvation
come.

Helen Keller

RESPONSORY

Ask, and it will be given you; seek and you will find. **—Ask**...
Knock, and it will be opened to you; **—seek**...
Glory to you, Source of all Being, Eternal Word and Holy Spirit.
—Ask...

CANTICLE

Ant Where your treasure is, there will your heart be also.

INTERCESSIONS:

As a youth, Jesus was found among the teachers in the
temple;
　　—strengthen the zeal of young women in their quest to grow
　　　in wisdom and holiness.
Many young women accepted martyrdom in times of
persecution;
　　—give courage to our young women today to be true to their

religious ideals and convictions when confronted by
conflicting values.

Jesus began his ministry at a wedding feast:
   —may the lives of our young women be joy-filled as they
   prepare for their careers and professions.

Our creation myth commissions us to be stewards of our
universe, to care for it and to tend it;
   —may our youth today learn to love and respect all creation,
   that the world they bequeath to their children will ensure
   a better quality of life.

We were created to know, love, and serve God;
   —give us the insight and the grace to understand that we
   do that best by knowing, loving, and serving one another
   in our families, in our communities, and with a concern
   for our sisters and brothers around the world.

PRAYER: O God, we give you thanks for our young
Christian women who so often delight and inspire
us. Give them all they need to be faithful to their
commitment. In difficult times, give them inner
peace and courage—but most of all hope and
trust that your will is for their happiness, and
that you are always faithful. May they come to
know you as Jesus did—a loving parent.
Especially we ask that you empower all young
women, that they may shape a world in which
they have equal opportunity and participation in
society and in the Church, that you may be well
served by all your children. We ask this in Jesus'
name. Amen.

DEATH OF A PARENT

MORNING/EVENING PRAYER

(Psalms for Death, p. 63 or p. 65)

Ant 1 Their good deeds have not been forgotten; their
prosperity will remain with their descendants.

Ant 2 Their posterity will continue forever, and their glory will not be blotted out.

Ant 3 Their bodies were buried in peace, and their name lives to all generations.

REFLECTION/SHARING

Since we believe that Jesus died and rose again, even so, through Jesus, God will bring with him those who have fallen asleep. For Christ will descend from heaven with a cry of command, with the archangel's call, and with the sound of the trumpet of God. And the dead in Christ will rise first; then we who are alive, who are left, shall be caught up together with them in the clouds to meet the Lord Jesus in the air; and so we shall always be with the Lord Jesus. Therefore comfort one another with these words.

(1 Thes 4:14, 16–18)

RESPONSORY

O God, you are my shepherd; I shall not want. —**O God**...
You make me to lie in green pastures; —**I shall**...
Glory to you Source of all Being, Eternal Word and Holy Spirit.
  —**O God**...

CANTICLE

Ant My soul is thirsting for God, the living God. When shall I come and see the face of God?

INTERCESSIONS:

When our parents die, part of us dies with them;
  —as they rise to eternal life, may we also experience resurrection as we mourn our loss.
Through our parents we have been blessed and we have been wounded;
  —help us to know reconciliation with our loved ones whether in this life or after they depart from us.
The love and care of our parents have surrounded us from our earliest years;

—may the memories we treasure enable us to be loving
and caring to those we serve.
We are part of who they were, both in our giftedness and our
woundedness;
—we give thanks for the gifts we have been given; help us to
forgive the hurts and enable us to be wounded healers.
Scripture tells us nothing of the deaths of Joseph or Mary;
—may those we love live on in our hearts and memories;
grant that we may all one day be together again.

PRAYER: O God, we know you as Mother and Father
through the mothers and fathers you have
given us. In them we have experienced your
unconditional love, your provident care, your
compassion, your availability to be the "for me"
in our lives. As they leave us to share fully in
eternal life with you, we feel a deep sense of loss
and emptiness. May our hearts know what our
faith believes, so that they may rejoice in the
knowledge that Jesus has overcome death and
that one day we will all be one in you. We ask
this through Jesus who is the Resurrection and
the Life. Amen.

DEATH OF A LOVED ONE

MORNING/EVENING PRAYER

(Psalms for Death, p. 63 or p. 65)

Ant 1 You have sorrow now, but I will see you again and
your hearts will rejoice, and no one will take your joy
from you.

Ant 2 I will come back and take you to myself, so that you
will be where I am.

Ant 3 I am the way, the truth, and the life.

REFLECTION/SHARING

As to separations, we may be sure that our hearts will always bleed for them; but that is the price we must pay for our loving God's entering into us a little further.

Teilhard de Chardin

RESPONSORY

Whether we live or die, we belong to the Lord. —**Whether**...
Christ died and rose to life in order to be the Lord of the
   living and the dead; —**we belong**...
Glory to you, Source of all Being, Eternal Word and Holy Spirit.
   —**Whether**...

CANTICLE

Ant Surely goodness and mercy shall follow me all the days
   of my life.

INTERCESSIONS:

In her grief, Martha said to Jesus: "If you had been here our brother would not have died";
   —let us know your consoling presence as we grieve for one
      we dearly love.
Jesus, you have overcome death—in death life is changed not taken away;
   —may we experience the resurrected life of _____
      in the communion of saints.
Death ends a life but not a relationship;
   —let us know that those we have loved are caring and
      available in a new way.
From your life-giving womb, O God, we were birthed into life;
   —comfort us as _____ is birthed into eternal life.
Help us to look toward death with a living hope;
   —we believe that the "day star" will rise in our hearts.

PRAYER: Jesus, you wept when you heard that Lazarus, your friend, had died. You know our pain and heartache when we lose someone very dear to us. Strengthen us at those times in our lives, and may the emptiness we feel turn to hope in resurrection and in the belief that we will one day be united again. We ask this in your name. Amen.

EMPOWERMENT

MORNING/EVENING PRAYER

(Psalms for Every Day, p. 71; Social Justice, p. 82)

Ant 1 I can do all things in the one who strengthens me.

Ant 2 My flesh and my heart may fail, but God is the strength of my heart and my portion forever.

Ant 3 It is God who goes before you, who will be with you, and will not fail you or forsake you; do not fear or be dismayed.

REFLECTION/SHARING

There is in Jerusalem by the Sheep Gate a pool which has five porticoes. In these lay a multitude of invalids, blind, lame, paralyzed. One was there, who had been ill for thirty-eight years. When Jesus saw her, he said, "Do you want to be healed?" The paralytic answered him, "Sir, I have no one to put me into the pool when the water is troubled." Jesus said to her, "Rise, take up your pallet and walk." And at once she was healed, and she took up her pallet and walked.

(Jn 3:18–19)

RESPONSORY

If our hearts do not condemn us, we have confidence in God.
 —**If our...**
We receive from God whatever we ask; —**we have...**
Glory to you, Source of all Being, Eternal Word and Holy Spirit.
 —**If our...**

CANTICLE

Ant With God, nothing will be impossible.

INTERCESSIONS:

Mary called Jesus forth at the wedding feast of Cana;
  —enable us to call forth the gifts and talents of others.
Mary Magdalene was given the mission to announce Jesus'
rising to his followers;
  —grant that women may be heard when they speak as the
    Spirit directs them.
The woman with a hemorrhage brought forth power from
Jesus with a touch;
  —may our reaching out to others empower them to be their
    true selves.
Miriam, the prophetess, led the people in dancing and singing
praises to God;
  —may women who are called be given the opportunity to
    lead the people of God according to their gifts.
Paul recognized Phoebe as deacon, sister, and patron;
  —grant that women be given equal compensation for their
    services and recognition of their achievements.

PRAYER: O God, your son, Jesus, defied the established
customs of his times in his willingness to relate
with women. He sat at their table, was taught by
them, and numbered them among his followers.
Throughout the ensuing centuries women have
been disregarded—often have been rendered
invisible and left unnamed. Remove the bushel
that has dimmed the light they have to give, and
enable them to shine forth in this our time, so
that this universe, your household, will be
glorified by all your daughters and sons—equal
participants in the salvific work of Jesus in
whose redemption we all partake. We ask this in
his name. Amen.

FOR MOTHER EARTH

MORNING/EVENING PRAYER

(Psalms for Creation, p. 59 or p. 61)

Ant 1 Behold the works of our God who has wrought wonders on the earth.

Ant 2 Nights and days, sing hymns of praise, light and darkness, lightnings and clouds.

Ant 3 Seas and rivers, dolphins and all water creatures, sing hymns of praise.

REFLECTION/SHARING

And God said, "Let the water under the heavens be gathered together into one place, and let the dry land appear." And God saw that it was good. And God said, "Let the earth put forth vegetation, plants yielding seed, and fruit trees bearing fruit in which is their seed, each according to its kind, upon the earth." And it was so. And God saw that it was good.

(Gen 1:9, 11–12)

RESPONSORY

You have established us to care for the creatures produced by you, to govern the world in holiness and justice. **—You**...
To render judgment in integrity of heart; **—to govern**...
Glory to you, Source of all Being, Eternal Word and Holy Spirit. **—You**...

CANTICLE

Ant Let birds of the air, beasts wild and tame, together with all living peoples, praise and exalt God above all forever.

INTERCESSIONS:

O God, you have given us seas, oceans, rivers, and lakes;
   —forgive our greed and negligence, which pollutes our waters and kills the life within them.

You placed us on a planet with an atmosphere that gives us air to breathe;
  —forgive us our production of toxic wastes and fuel emissions, and for our reluctance to sacrifice our comforts for cleaner air.
The earth cannot survive without our rain forests;
  —forgive our consumerism, which has caused the destruction of so many of them, inflicting violence on native peoples and animals who dwell there.
Animals, large and small, roam our forests and jungles and swim in our oceans;
  —forgive us for causing the extinction of so many species and for our silence in the face of poaching and inhumane fishing methods.
You created the heavens and the earth and have given this earth to us as our home;
  —grant that we and all peoples will show our gratitude by the care and respect we give to all that you have made.

PRAYER: Gracious God, open our hearts and eyes to the wonders of your presence among us in all forms of being. Help us to reach beyond ourselves so that our love and concern embraces all creation that shares this universe with us: peoples of every nation, animals of every species, all forms of vegetation, the planets, stars, and all the elements. We pray this in union with the incarnate Word of God in whose image all was created. May you be blessed throughout the ages and for all eternity. Amen.

FOR PREGNANT MOTHERS
MORNING/EVENING PRAYER
(Psalms for Mothers, p. 81)

Ant 1 Hail, Mary, full of grace. Blessed is the fruit of your womb.

Ant 2 Hannah pleaded with the Most High, and a child was
conceived in her womb.

Ant 3 When Elizabeth heard the greeting of Mary, the babe
leaped in her womb.

REFLECTION/SHARING

Tobit called Tobias to him and said, "My son, when I die,
bury me, and do not neglect your mother. Honor her all the
days of your life; do what is pleasing to her, and do not
grieve her. Remember, my son, that she faced many dangers
for you while you were yet unborn." (Tob 4:3–4)

RESPONSORY

You formed my inward parts, you knit me together in my
   mother's womb. **—You formed**...
My frame was not hidden from you; **—you knit**...
Glory to you, Source of all Being, Eternal Word and Holy Spirit.
   —You formed...

CANTICLE

Ant Let your mother and father be glad; let her who bore
   you rejoice.

INTERCESSIONS:

As Sarah longed for Isaac;
   —let the longing for this child increase the longing in
      our hearts that it be another incarnation, a word of God
      enfleshed among us.
As Hannah longed for Samuel;
   —may this baby grow in strength nourished both by love
      and the good health of its mother.
As Elizabeth rejoiced in the babe in her womb;
   —may this child leap with joy and may it encounter the life
      of Jesus in all those who care for it.
As Mary waited in mystery and longing;
   —may this expectant mother experience the joy of bringing
      a new child of God into the world.

As we pray both for the baby and for its mother;
—grant that we may work for a world where the future is
secure and where justice is experienced by all.

PRAYER: O God, you have gifted this woman with a fruitful
womb, and we live in expectation for the life that
is to be born. As we await its coming we give
thanks to you for bringing us and all creatures
on this earth to birth. May your mothering care
and unconditional love enable this expectant
mother to care for her child as you care for us.
May this new child come to know, love, and serve
you as did Jesus, who is its companion on the
journey home to you. We ask this in his name.
Amen.

HOMELESS WOMEN AND CHILDREN

MORNING/EVENING PRAYER

(Psalms for Social Justice, p. 82; Times of Distress, p. 67)

Ant 1 Foxes have holes, and birds of the air have nests; but
the Anointed One has nowhere to lay his head.

Ant 2 O God, you have been our dwelling place in all
generations; from everlasting to everlasting you are
God.

Ant 3 With your faithful help, O God, rescue me; let not the
flood sweep over me or the deep swallow me up.

REFLECTION/SHARING

Is not this the fast that I choose, says the Most High:
to loose the bonds of wickedness,
to let the oppressed go free,
and to break every yoke?
Is it not to share your bread with the hungry,
and bring the homeless poor into your house? (Is 58:6, 7–9)

RESPONSORY

I looked, and there was no one to help. **—I looked**...
I was appalled, but there was no one to uphold me;
  —and there...
Glory to you, Source of all Being, Eternal Word and Holy Spirit.
  —I looked...

CANTICLE

Ant Because you have made God your refuge, the Most
      High your habitation, no evil shall befall you.

INTERCESSIONS:

Menial job, inadequate pay to afford room and shelter;
  —give us eyes to see the injustice of an inadequate wage
    that does not provide for ordinary human needs.
Belongings in bags and carts, no space to call one's own;
  —enable us to create systems of government that ensure
    every person a decent place to live.
Women living in shelters, sleeping in cars, bathing in public
bathrooms;
  —these are our sisters, our family—all of us children
    of God.
Children with empty stomachs, no place to play, nowhere to do
homework;
  —these are our future, our hope for the world.
We sing: "Be it ever so humble, there's no place like home";
  —forgive us for we know not what we do, but our hearts and
    voices cry out for justice. Show us the way.

PRAYER: O God, we live in a world where a few have too
          much and so many have nothing—not even a
          place to lay their head. We pray especially for
          those most vulnerable, for the women and
          children who are victims of legislation that
          ignores their needs, of bureaucracy that is too
          regimented to act, of systems that fail to see into
          the eyes of this individual person. Enlighten us
          that we may do what little we can to create a

world where all have what they need to live their
lives with dignity and self-respect. We ask this in
Jesus' name. Amen.

IN THE NURSING HOME

MORNING/EVENING PRAYER

(Psalms for the Aging, p. 57)

Ant 1 Jesus said to Peter, "Truly, truly, I say to you, when
you were young, you girded yourself and walked
where you would; but when you are old, you will
stretch out your hands, and another will gird you
and carry you where you do not wish to go."

Ant 2 People were bringing a paralyzed man, and sought to
lay him before Jesus; but finding no way to bring him
in, they went up on the roof and let him down with
his bed through the tiles into the midst before Jesus.

Ant 3 There was a woman who had a spirit of infirmity for
eighteen years; she was bent over and could not fully
straighten herself. When Jesus saw her, he called her
and said to her, "Woman, you are freed from your
infirmity."

REFLECTION/SHARING

Do not disregard the discourse of the aged,
for they themselves learned from their ancestors;
because from them you will gain understanding
and learn how to give an answer in time of need. (Sir 8:9)

RESPONSORY

Even to old age and gray hairs, O God, do not forsake me.
  —**Even**...
Till I proclaim your might to all the generations to come;
  —**O God**...
Glory to you, Source of all Being, Eternal Word and Holy Spirit.
  —**Even**...

CANTICLE

Ant O God, forsake me not when my strength is spent.

INTERCESSIONS:

Canes, walkers, wheelchairs;
   —we give thanks, O God, for aids that promote our mobility.
Sad eyes, twinkling eyes, vacant eyes;
   —give us the vision to see and reverence the sacred journey
   that these eyes have witnessed.
Frail hands, bony hands, trembling hands;
   —bless all they have touched and transform it as Jesus
   transformed water into wine.
Bed rails, chair straps, leg braces;
   —may all whose bodies are restrained to their respective
   crosses, like Jesus, experience the freedom of a life-giving
   spirit.
Gentle words, silent words, bitter words;
   —unite them as one unending song of praise for lives that
   have lived the many cycles of life, death, and resurrection.

PRAYER: O God, we give you thanks for mystery that calls
upon our faith to acknowledge human limitations
as your gift to us. In the evening of our lives,
enable us to surrender and give back to you all
that life requires of us. Bless all those who care
for and serve those unable to help themselves,
and may we each know the gift of serving and
being served. We ask this through Jesus who is
our companion on the way. Amen.

IN TIMES OF DISTRESS

MORNING/EVENING PRAYER

(Psalms in Times of Distress, p. 67 or p. 69)

Ant 1 O God, give ear to my prayer; hide not from my supplication!

Ant 2 Attend to me and answer me; I am overcome by my troubles.

Ant 3 My heart is in anguish within me, the terrors of death fall upon me.

REFLECTION/SHARING

In this you rejoice, though now for a little while you may have to suffer various trials, so that the genuineness of your faith, more precious than gold, which though perishable is tested by fire, may redound to praise and glory and honor at the revelation of Jesus Christ. Without having seen him, you love him; though you do not now see him, you believe in him and rejoice with unutterable and exalted joy. As the outcome of your faith, you obtain salvation of your souls.

(1 Pet 1:6–9)

RESPONSORY

O that I had wings like a dove; I would fly away and be at rest. **—O that...**
I would haste to find me a shelter; **—I would...**
Glory to you, Source of all Being, Eternal Word and Holy Spirit. **—O that...**

CANTICLE

Ant Cast your burdens on God, and you will be supported.

INTERCESSIONS:

You alone, O God, are my rock and my stronghold;
   —enable us to cling to you when all else seems hopeless.
Evening, morning, and at noon I utter complaint and lament;
   —hear our cries and answer our pleas.

In you alone is my deliverance, my refuge;
   —increase our faith and trust; to whom else can we go?
Restore us, O God, let your face shine upon us that we may be
saved;
   —comfort us in our affliction.
Our help comes from you, O God, who made heaven and
earth;
   —deliver our eyes from tears and our feet from stumbling.

PRAYER: O God, our hearts are heavily burdened, but we
come to you remembering the words of Jesus:
Come to me all who labor and are heavy laden,
and I will give you rest. Help us at this time and
give us the peace that the world cannot give. As
you suffered with Jesus upon the cross, be with
us now and help us to be totally open to your will
as Jesus was. We ask this in his name. Amen.

JUBILEE OF RELIGIOUS PROFESSION

MORNING/EVENING PRAYER

Ant 1 I seek your face, O God, and yearn for you.

Psalm 63:1–9

O God, you are my God, I
long for you;
my soul thirsts for you;
My body seeks for you
as in a dry and weary land
without water.
So I have looked upon you
in the sanctuary,
beholding your power and
your glory.

For your constant love is
better than life,—

my lips will sing your
praises.
So I will bless you as long
as I live;
I will lift up my hands and
call on your name.

My soul feasts on you and
my mouth praises you,
as I think of you upon my
bed,
and meditate on you in the
watches of the night;
for you have been my help.
In the shadow of your
wings I sing for joy.—

My soul clings to you; your hand upholds me.

Glory to you Source of all Being, Eternal Word and Holy Spirit.

As it was in the beginning, is now and will be forever. Amen.

Ant 2 We shall go up with joy to the house of our God.

Psalm 84

How lovely is your dwelling place,
O God of hosts!

My soul longs and yearns for the courts of the Most High;
my heart and lips sing for joy
to you the living God.

Even the sparrow finds a home,
and the swallow a nest for its brood,
where it may lay its young, at your altars, O God!

Blessed are those who dwell in your house,
for ever singing your praise!
Blessed are those whose strength you are,
in whose hearts are the roads to Zion.

O God, hear my prayer;
give ear, O God of our ancestors!
Look upon our shield, O God;
look on the face of your anointed!

For one day in your courts is better,
than a thousand anywhere else.
I would rather stand at your threshold,
than dwell in the tents of wickedness.

For you are a sun and a shield;
you bestow favor and honor.
No good do you withhold from those who walk uprightly.

O God! God Most High!
Blessed are those who trust in you!

Glory to you Source of all Being, Eternal Word and Holy Spirit.

As it was in the beginning, is now and will be forever. Amen.

Ant 3 How can I repay you, O God, for your goodness to me?

Psalm 8

How great is your name, O
  God,
in all the earth!

You whose glory above the
  heavens
is chanted on the lips of
  babes,
have founded a defense
  against your foes,
to silence the cries of the
  rebels.

When I look at the
  heavens,
the work of your hands,
the moon and the stars
  which you established;
who are we that you
  should keep us in mind?
mortal flesh that you care
  for us?

Yet you have made us little
  less than God,
and crowned us with glory
  and honor.
You entrust us with the
  works of your hands,
to care for all creation.

All sheep and oxen,
and even the beasts of the
  field,
the birds of the air, and
  the fish of the sea,
whatever passes along the
  paths of the sea.

How great is your name,
  Creator God,
in all the earth!

Glory to you Source of all
  Being, Eternal Word and
  Holy Spirit.

As it was in the beginning,
  is now and will be
  forever. Amen.

REFLECTION/SHARING

You shall hallow the fiftieth year, and proclaim liberty
throughout the land to all its inhabitants; it shall be a
jubilee for you, when each of you shall return to her property
and each of you shall return to your family.... You shall
neither sow, nor reap what grows of itself, nor gather the
grapes from the undressed vines. For it is a jubilee; it shall
be holy to you.... (Lev 25:10, 11, 12)

RESPONSORY

You did not choose me, but I chose you. —**You did**...
That you should go and bear fruit; —**I chose**...

Glory to you, Source of all Being, Eternal Word and Holy Spirit.
—You did...

CANTICLE

Ant For you, who are mighty, have made me great. Most Holy be your Name.

INTERCESSIONS:

O God, we thank you for the gift of our Sister _____ and for the many years she has served our community;
   —bless her this day and grant that this year may be a jubilee year of grace.
We thank you for her parents and for all those who nurtured and gifted her;
   —may they share the joy of this day with all the communion of saints both here on earth and with life in you.
This day marks a milestone in the life of our Sister, _____ .
   —may her journey that is yet to be, continue to reflect the good news which Jesus proclaimed.
We bring to mind our family, friends, and all who share in this celebration;
   —grant that each receive the grace to be faithful to their own personal commitments.
The joy of this jubilee touches our world as a salvific event;
   —may our participation in our cosmos always bring it to a better quality of life.

PRAYER: O God, we thank you for the gift of this day and for all days that remind us of your faithful covenant with us. Grant that this jubilee may be a year of favor to our Sister, _____ , and that all may share in it so that our world may know peace, the hungry be fed, and the poor share the bounty of our earth. We ask this in the name of Jesus who proclaimed good news to all God's people. Amen.

LIVING ALONE

(Psalms for Every Day, p. 71 or p. 73)

MORNING/EVENING PRAYER

Ant 1 I will allure her and bring her into the wilderness and speak tenderly to her.

Ant 2 Where shall I go from your Spirit? Or where shall I flee from your presence?

Ant 3 God is my rock and my salvation.

REFLECTION/SHARING

Then Jesus made the disciples get into the boat and go before him to the other side, while he dismissed the crowds. And after he had dismissed the crowds, he went up on the mountain by himself to pray. When evening came, he was there alone. (Mt 14:22, 23)

RESPONSORY

For God alone my soul waits in silence. —**For God...**
I shall not be shaken; —**my soul...**
Glory to you, Source of all Being, Eternal Word and Holy Spirit.
   —**For God...**

CANTICLE

Ant How lovely is your dwelling place, O God, my God.

INTERCESSIONS:

Jesus left his home in Nazareth and went into the desert;
   —help us when we are alone to use our solitude creatively and fruitfully.
Jesus reached out to the poor and to the outcast;
   —make us aware of the needs of our neighbors where we live and where we work.
When we find ourselves burdened by hectic demands on our time;
   —may the solitude of our dwelling place be a solace and comfort.

When we experience feelings of loneliness and restlessness;
  —transform our emptiness into the fullness of your presence
  and quiet our minds so that we may know your
  companionship.
When we have no one to share our joys and sorrows;
  —enable us to unite this form of poverty with all those who
  find themselves alone or abandoned. May this emptiness
  know your creative power.

PRAYER: O God, your son, Jesus, told us that the foxes
have dens and the birds of the air have nests,
but that he had nowhere to lay his head. Give
us a grateful heart for providing us with this
space—our own small corner of the world where
we live. Bless it and make it holy, and enable us
to serve you more faithfully and lovingly because
you are ever Emmanuel—God with us. We ask
this in Jesus' name. Amen.

LIVING with a LIFE-THREATENING DISEASE

(Psalms for Every Day, p. 71; Times of Distress, p. 67)

MORNING/EVENING PRAYER

Ant 1 Christ Jesus, if you will, you can make me whole.

Ant 2 Say but the word, and we shall be healed.

Ant 3 You, O God, can rebuild what was destroyed and
replant what was ruined.

REFLECTION/SHARING

When Jesus and his disciples had got out of the boat,
immediately the people recognized Jesus, and ran about the
whole neighborhood and began to bring sick people on their
pallets to any place where they heard he was. And wherever
he came, in villages, cities, or country, they laid the sick in
the marketplaces, and besought him that they might touch
even the fringe of his garment; and as many as touched it
were made well. (Jn 11:21–27)

RESPONSORY

I set before you life and death, blessing and curse; therefore
   choose life. —**I set...**
That you may dwell in the land I promised you; —**choose...**
Glory to you, Source of all Being, Eternal Word and Holy Spirit.
   —**I set...**

CANTICLE

Ant I was often severely hindered by sickness and involved
   with heavy sufferings that threatened to bring me to
   death's door. And yet God has always made me alive
   again, even to this day. (Hildegard of Bingen)

INTERCESSIONS:

O God, each day and every moment comes from you as gift;
   —enable us to live fully in the present, cherishing the
     moment that is now ours.
Your son, Jesus, told us not to be anxious about the needs
of each day, for your loving care is with us;
   —quiet our fears about the future and give us the gift of
     inner peace.
Peter was told he would be led by a path not of his own
choosing;
   —help us to surrender to the way you are leading us and
     give us the gift of trust.
Jesus, you healed the woman who touched your garment;
   —give us the faith to believe in the healing we need to
     fully participate in your salvific work.
As you hung upon the cross, some jeered, "He saved others,
himself he cannot save";
   —do not let us give up hope when all seems lost.

PRAYER: O God, the day you birthed us into being is the
        day we began our journey back to you. You are
        with us every step of the way. Give us the grace to
        embrace our journey with joy and appreciation.
        Help us to see the beauty around us—the beauty
        of nature and the beauty of friendships. Let our

gratitude for all your gifts make us ever aware of your presence and love for us. Especially do we thank you for our brother, Jesus, who found peace in your will when his hour drew near. Amen.

LIVING WITH ORDINARY ROUTINE

(Psalms for Every Day, p. 71 or p. 73)

MORNING/EVENING PRAYER

Ant 1 Though he was in the form of God, Jesus did not count equality with God something to be grasped at; but emptied himself, taking the form of a slave, being born in human likeness.

Ant 2 In the morning, fill us with your love, that we may rejoice and be glad all our days: give success to the work of our hands.

Ant 3 You will show me the path of life; in your presence there is fullness of joy; in your hands, happiness forever.

REFLECTION/SHARING

Being fully human is the first response that we can make to God's seeking us. Being human is the first condition for becoming divine.

RESPONSORY

The eyes of all creatures look to you, to give them their
    food in due season. **—The eyes...**
You open wide your hand and satisfy the desires of every
    living thing; **—to give...**
Glory to you, Source of all Being, Eternal Word and Holy Spirit.
    —The eyes...

CANTICLE

Ant Every day I will bless you, and praise your name
forever.

INTERCESSIONS:

Give us awareness, O God, to experience the miracle of your
presence in our everyday world;
    —for it is in you that we live and move and have our being.
God, you are the giver of peace;
    —quiet our minds so that we can notice your presence all
    around us in what is seemingly ordinary.
You are the giver of life;
    —let us be as children, alive and present to the newness and
    freshness of every moment.
Jesus, in our fast-paced, neon-lit, high-stimuli world;
    —help us to walk in simplicity with you.
When we cannot see your wonder, O God, as we struggle in
the marketplace;
    —give us the strength to endure and to hope, and to be
    compassionate with ourselves.

PRAYER: O God, open our eyes to see your beauty and
wonder within daily sights as simple as a sink
full of sunshine and water and swirling, green
spinach leaves. Help us see beyond our veiled
vision so that we may behold the abidingly
beautiful reflection of you in the eyes of a baby,
spouse or friend. May we feel your presence in
the magic of our breathing. We ask this in the
name of our teacher, Jesus, who will show us
these things and more. Amen.

LOSS OF A CHILD

(Psalms for Death, p. 63; Times of Distress, p. 67)

MORNING/EVENING PRAYER

Ant 1 A voice was heard in Ramah, wailing and loud lamentation, Rachel weeping for her children, because they were no more.

Ant 2 King David cried with a loud voice: "O my son Absalom, O Absalom, my son, my son!"

Ant 3 Is it nothing to you, all you who pass by? Look and see if there is any sorrow like my sorrow which was brought upon me.

REFLECTION/SHARING

As Jesus drew near to the gate of the city, behold, a man who had died was being carried out, the only son of his mother, and she was a widow; and a large crowd from the city was with her. And when the Lord saw her, he had compassion on her and said to her, "Do not weep." And he came and touched the bier. (Lk 7:12–13)

RESPONSORY

As one whom a mother comforts, so I will comfort you;
   —As one...
You shall see, and your heart shall rejoice; **—so I...**
Glory to you, Source of all Being, Eternal Word and Holy Spirit.
   —As one...

CANTICLE

Ant Lift up your eyes round about and see; they all gather together, they come to you; your sons shall come from afar, and your daughters shall be carried in your arms.

INTERCESSIONS:

Ruth supported Naomi who wept for her sons;
   —may we experience the comfort of those who love us.

Mary and Joseph searched for the boy, Jesus;
  —grant hope to those who seek for a missing loved one.
Jesus had compassion on the widow of Naim;
  —comfort parents who grieve the death of a child.
Jesus raised the daughter of Jairus;
  —may our faith in the resurrection bring solace to all those who mourn.
Mary stood under the cross of her crucified son;
  —may she intercede for all mothers whose children are victims of injustice or violence.

PRAYER: O God, you give and you take away. Our hearts grieve that one we loved was with us but a short time. We do not understand your ways, but we believe in your love. May this child who now lives with you be your delight, and may we one day be reunited that we may know again the joy of being together. We ask this in the name of Jesus who now lives with you for all eternity. Amen.

LOVE AND FRIENDSHIP

(Psalms for Every Day, p. 71 or p. 73)

MORNING/EVENING PRAYER

Ant 1 A faithful friend is a sturdy shelter; she that has found one, has found a treasure.

Ant 2 There is nothing so precious as a faithful friend, and no scales can measure her excellence.

Ant 3 There is no greater love than to lay down one's life for a friend.

REFLECTION/SHARING

We must always be more or less lonely, but sometimes it is given to spirit to touch spirit—then we understand and are understood.

                                    Janet Erskine Stuart

RESPONSORY

This is my commandment, that you love one another.
  —This is...
As I have loved you; **—love one...**
Glory to you, Source of all Being, Eternal Word and Holy Spirit.
  —This is...

CANTICLE

Ant Love bears all things, believes all things, hopes all
  things, endures all things.

INTERCESSIONS:

A true and loyal friend is a precious and rare gift;
  —we thank you, O God, for the friends you have given us.
Through mutual sharing we discover our true selves;
  —give us true self-knowledge and let us be grateful
  to those who help us attain it.
A grateful memory keeps lifelong friendships ever new;
  —may we cherish the past, enjoy the present, and
  anticipate the future with joy.
There is no greater love than to give one's life for a friend;
  —we bless you for the many times our friends have given
  their time, their energy, their very lives for us.
You long to call us friends;
  —may the love friends have for each other be generative for
  the good of all they touch and for society as a whole.

PRAYER: Lord Jesus, we are all God's children and we are
  all your friends. We are particularly grateful
  today for those special people you have put into
  our lives who share our hopes and dreams. As we
  continue our journey together toward holiness
  and wholeness, may you walk with us as you did
  with your friends on the way to Emmaus. Let us
  recognize you when we break bread together and
  know you as our companion on the way. We ask
  this in your name. Amen.

MARRIAGE

MORNING/EVENING PRAYER

(Psalms for Feasts, p. 75, or p. 77)

Ant 1 As bride and groom rejoice in one another, so shall your God rejoice in you.

Ant 2 Set me as a seal upon your heart, as a seal upon your arm; for love is strong as death.

Ant 3 As therefore you received Christ Jesus the Lord, so live in him, rooted and built up in him and established in the faith, abounding in thanksgiving.

REFLECTION/SHARING

Love must strive to give itself totally. Until this fundamental act of self-renunciation has been made, love must remain precarious, for its continuance will depend upon such factors as states of mind, thoughts of return, demonstrations of affections, all or any of which may fail at any moment.... A sense of insecurity in love cannot be met by tangible proofs of affection; we find the only answer to love's problem is to love more.

Author Unknown

RESPONSORY

I will sing of loyalty and of justice; to you, O God, I will sing.
—**I will**...
I will walk with integrity of heart within my house; —**to you**...
Glory to you, Source of all Being, Eternal Word and Holy Spirit.
—**I will**...

CANTICLE

Ant Make love your aim, and earnestly desire the spiritual gifts.

INTERCESSIONS:

Jesus prayed that we may be one even as he is one with God;

—may the union of husband and wife foster the unique gifts
and individuality of each partner.
You told us that we are not servants but friends;
—grant that the joys and trials shared together enable each
to be best friend to the other.
You call us friends because you have revealed to us all you
have learned from God;
—support wives and husbands through difficult situations
and enable them to share their feelings and concerns with
one another in love and mutual respect.
Those who abide in love abide in God;
—help married couples to abide in love as love evolves from
attraction to commitment.
We are called to be happy in this world as well as in the world
to come;
—grant that wives and husbands grow in joy as they journey
through life together.

PRAYER: O God, your son Jesus began his ministry at a
wedding celebration. May the joy that is
experienced as two people begin a life together
continue to grow and deepen through all that life
has to offer along the way. May Jesus continue to
transform the water of their every day to the wine
of new vision so that what seems ordinary
becomes transformed by love. May couples grow
old together knowing the best wine is saved till
last and that Jesus is the abiding guest and their
companion on the way. We ask this in Jesus'
name. Amen.

MOTHERS

MORNING/EVENING PRAYER

(Psalms for Mothers, p. 81)

Ant 1 Whoever glorifies their mother is like one who lays up
treasure.

Ant 2 Those who obey God will refresh their mother.

Ant 3 Reject not your mother's teaching, for it is a fair
garland for your head and a pendant for your neck.

REFLECTION/SHARING

A Canaanite woman from that region came out and cried,
"Have mercy on me, O Lord, Son of David; my daughter is
severely possessed by a demon." Jesus answered, "I was
sent only to the lost sheep of the house of Israel. It is not fair
to take the children's bread and throw it to the dogs." She
said, "Yes, Lord, yet even the dogs eat the crumbs that fall
from their masters' table." Then Jesus answered her, "O
woman, great is your faith! Be it done for you as you desire."
                                        (Mt 15:22, 24, 26–28)

RESPONSORY

As one whom a mother comforts, so I will comfort you;
    —**As one**...
You shall see, and your heart shall rejoice; —**so I**...
Glory to you, Source of all Being, Eternal Word and Holy Spirit.
    —**As one**...

CANTICLE

Ant Mary gave birth to her firstborn son and wrapped him
in swaddling cloths and laid him in a manger, because
there was no place for them in the inn.

INTERCESSIONS:

O God, you gave us these valiant women to image your
unconditional love;
    —may we become selfless and giving in our relationships
    with others.
As you blessed them with wisdom;
    —help us to grow in the knowledge of your ways.
They cared for our physical, psychological, and spiritual well-
being;
    —support us in our efforts to reach out to others in need.

You placed Jesus in the care of Mary;
  —may we always give thanks for those you have given to us
    as our primary nurturers.
Mary stood beneath the cross of Jesus;
  —give us the courage of our mothers that we, too, may be
    faithful in love.

PRAYER: Loving God, you, who birthed all into being,
created women to be life-givers. We thank you for
our mothers and our mothers' mothers. In pain
and joy they gave us life, nurtured us, and
imaged your loving care. Enable us to be for
those who follow us, what they have been for
us—that others may see you as our God, our
Mother, our life-giving Source, our holy-available
One. We ask this through Jesus, your son and
our brother. Amen.

FOR WIDOWS OF SLAIN HUSBANDS

MORNING/EVENING PRAYER

(Psalms for Death, p. 63; Times of Distress, p. 67)

Ant 1 Thus says the God of hosts: Render true judgments,
show kindness and mercy, do not oppress the widow,
the orphan, or the poor.

Ant 2 Jesus said, "Truly, I say to you, this poor widow has
put in more than all those who are contributing to
the treasury; she has put in everything she had."

Ant 3 The widow, Anna, gave thanks to God, and spoke of
Jesus to all who were looking for the redemption of
Jerusalem.

REFLECTION/SHARING

God will not ignore the supplication of the fatherless,
nor the widow when she pours out her story.
Do not the tears of the widow run down her cheek

as she cries out against those who caused them to fall?
The prayer of the humble pierces the clouds,
and one will not be consoled until it reaches the Most High.

(Sir 35:14–15, 17)

RESPONSORY

God is the protector of widows, giving the desolate a home to
  dwell in. **—God is...**
Leading out prisoners to prosperity; **—giving...**
Glory to you, Source of all Being, Eternal Word and Holy Spirit.
  —God is...

CANTICLE

Ant When Jesus saw the widow, he had compassion on her
  and said to her, "Do not weep."

INTERCESSIONS:

O God, the ravages of war are death and destruction;
  —comfort women whose husbands or loved ones never
    returned to share their lives.
Our cities and highways know crime and violence;
  —may widows of police officers find the support they need
    to bear their loss.
Firefighters risk their lives daily;
  —ease the suffering of wives and mothers whose husbands
    and sons gave their lives in perilous situations.
Accidents, unsafe work environments, unseen circumstances
cause death and grief.
  —may women who have known such grief also know the
    comfort and peace that only you can give.
Each day lives are lost by random acts of violence;
  —through the care of family and friends, encircle with your
    ever-present love women whose husbands have been
    killed.

PRAYER: O God, through the death of your son, Jesus, you
  know the grief of those who have lost a loved one
  in such a violent way. We cannot understand the

mystery of life or death, but help us to accept it in faith and to believe in your provident love and care. As those we loved are now with you, may they also be with us, interceding on our behalf. We ask this in the name of our crucified Jesus, who overcame death and now lives with you for all eternity. Amen.

WOMEN AS SINGLE PARENTS
MORNING/EVENING PRAYER
(Psalms for Every Day, p. 71; Times of Distress, p. 67)

Ant 1 Behold, I create new heavens and a new earth; I will be glad in my people; they shall not labor in vain or bear children for calamity.

Ant 2 I will strengthen you, I will help you, I will uphold you with my victorious hand.

Ant 3 I will contend with those who will contend with you, and I will save your children.

REFLECTION/SHARING

I will feed my flock like a shepherd,
I will gather the lambs in my arms,
I will carry them in my bosom,
and gently lead those that are with young. (Is 49:25–26)

RESPONSORY

Turn to me, O God, and take pity on me. —**Turn to**...
Give your strength to your servant; save the child of your
   handmaid, —**and take**...
Glory to you, Source of all Being, Eternal Word and Holy Spirit.
   —**Turn to**...

CANTICLE

Ant God is my shepherd, I shall not want; I fear no evil, for
   God is with me.

INTERCESSIONS:

God, you are both Mother and Father to us;
   —help those women who have sole responsibility of both
   mothering and fathering their children.
You have given us plants and animals that nourish us, yet
many go hungry;
   —enable working mothers to earn adequate income for the
   sustenance and nurturing of their children.
In the mystery of the Trinity, you reveal yourself as a God of
relationship;
   —may single mothers know friendships through which they
   may share their burdens and concerns as well as their
   joys.
Jesus welcomed the presence of children;
   —give working mothers the wisdom and patience they need,
   especially when they are tired and overburdened.
Jesus chided those in authority who laid heavy burdens on the
poor and oppressed;
   —grant that governments provide legislation that ensures
   equal recompense to women for equal services, recognizing
   that women share equal burdens.

PRAYER: O God, your son Jesus lived among us sharing
   our burdens and concerns. You know well the
   difficulties and anxieties of women who have sole
   care of their children. Enable them to be good
   providers and comfort them in their trials. May
   they share fully in your Motherhood and
   Fatherhood so that their children will know
   themselves as your children, secure in your
   provident love. We ask this in Jesus' name.
   Amen.

WOMEN IN PRISON

MORNING/EVENING PRAYER

(Psalms for Social Justice, p. 82; Times of Distress, p. 67)

Ant 1 Out of the depths I cry to you, O God, hear my voice!

Ant 2 With you is found forgiveness; for this we revere you.

Ant 3 With you, O God, there is love, and fullness of redemption.

REFLECTION/SHARING

[Jesus] came to Nazareth, where he had been brought up; and he went to the synagogue, as his custom was, on the sabbath day. And he stood up to read; and there was given to him the book of the prophet Isaiah. He opened the book and found the place where it was written, "The Spirit of the Most High is upon me, because God has anointed me to preach good news to the poor; to proclaim release to the captives, and recovering of sight to the blind, to set at liberty those who are oppressed, to proclaim the acceptable year of the Most High." He closed the book, and gave it back to the attendant, and sat down; and the eyes of all in the synagogue were fixed on him. He began to say to them, "Today this scripture has been fulfilled in your hearing." (Lk 4:16–21)

RESPONSORY

Have mercy on me, O God, according to your steadfast love.
 —Have mercy...
Create in me a clean heart; **—according...**
Glory to you, Source of all Being, Eternal Word and Holy Spirit.
 —Have mercy...

CANTICLE

Ant With God on our side, who can be against us?

INTERCESSIONS:

All-merciful God, you see the depths of every heart;
  —grant peace to the minds and hearts of women in prison;
    help them to face the reality of their situation with courage
    and hope.
Whatever the cause of their bondage;
  —set their spirits free to follow in the footsteps of Jesus—
    the way of the gospel, the way of faith, love, and goodness.
Protect them from the dangers within the prison walls;
  —grant them the courage of a Judith and Esther, and other
    faith-filled women who have taught us the blessing of
    trusting in your constant protection.
Christ Jesus, you longed to gather your people to you as a
mother hen gathers her young;
  —show your tender compassion to women in prison who
    must remain childless and to mothers who yearn and fear
    for their children. Be Mother to them all.
When prisoners are absent from family celebrations or from
memorial services for their departed loved ones;
  —give them and their families and friends a heroic faith in
    your resurrection and their own—day by day.

PRAYER: "I am never alone, for God is always with me."
         Jesus, let your words echo in the hearts of
         women as they face the loneliness of prison life.
         Be their fullness in times of privation; let your
         Spirit within them rise with gifts of patience in
         times of disappointment and with comfort in
         times of anguish. Let no humiliation make them
         forget their dignity as children of God, created in
         the divine image. Help us to know how to enable
         them to persevere in faith and to grow in your
         love. We ask this in your name. Amen.

WOMEN IN PROFESSIONAL CAREERS

MORNING/EVENING PRAYER

(Psalms for Every Day, p. 71 or p. 73)

Ant 1 Make me know your ways, O God; teach me your paths. Lead me in your truth and teach me.

Ant 2 I bless God who counsels me; in the night also my heart instructs me.

Ant 3 O God, let your good spirit lead me in ways that are level and smooth.

REFLECTION/SHARING

On the sabbath day we went outside the gate to the riverside, where we supposed there was a place of prayer; and we sat down and spoke to the women who had come together. One who had heard us was a woman named Lydia, from the city of Thyatira, a seller of purple goods, who was a worshiper of God. The Lord opened her heart to give heed to what was said by Paul. (Acts 16:13–15)

RESPONSORY

O God, give us wisdom, the attendant at your throne, that
   she may be with us and work with us. **—O God...**
Send her forth from your holy heavens; **—that she...**
Glory to you, Source of all Being, Eternal Word and Holy Spirit.
   —O God...

CANTICLE

Ant Truly I say to you, unless you turn and become like children, you will never enter the realm of heaven.

INTERCESSIONS:

Phoebe was a deacon in the early Church; Bridget of Kildare, who was a Druid priestess, continued her priestly ministry as a Christian and abbess;
   —bless women theologians today, and may their work enable women to take their rightful place in church ministry and leadership.

Queen Esther pleaded eloquently the cause of her people
before King Assuerus;
  —we give thanks for women in the legal professions and
    pray that justice be better served through them.
People from all over the countryside came to Hildegard of
Bingen because of her knowledge of medicinal herbs and her
power of healing;
  —may women in health professions share in the healing
    power of Jesus, combining their scientific knowledge with
    true compassion.
Through her writings, Teresa of Avila was declared a Doctor of
the Church;
  —grant women poets, writers, and journalists the power to
    express and to articulate their findings and experience, so
    that women's reality may enter the mainstream of history.
Women throughout the centuries have been great educators;
they have managed business affairs and households and
excelled in specialized fields;
  —empower women seeking professional occupations to
    achieve equal opportunity and just recompense for their
    services.

PRAYER: O God, you have created us in your image and
             have endowed all people with intelligence,
             talents, the ability to dream dreams, and the
             hope to follow them. Too often women have been
             denied opportunities to follow their dreams and
             your calling. Remove the obstacles that stand in
             the way of justice, so that this world may better
             serve you by using the gifts and talents you have
             given each one. We ask this in the name of Jesus
             who died for the liberation of us all. Amen.

WOMEN SEEKING OR SERVING IN POLITICAL OFFICE

MORNING/EVENING PRAYER

(Psalms for Every Day, p. 71; Feasts, p. 75)

Ant 1 Deborah, a prophetess...was judging Israel at that time. She used to sit under the palm of Deborah, and the people of Israel came up to her for judgment.

Ant 2 Uzziah said to Judith, "O daughter, may God grant this to be a perpetual honor to you, because you did not spare your own life when our nation was brought low."

Ant 3 There was a wedding in Cana of Galilee, and the mother of Jesus was there. When the wine gave out, she said to him, "They have no wine."

REFLECTION/SHARING

The peasantry ceased in Israel, they ceased until you arose, Deborah,
arose as a mother in Israel.
My heart goes out to the commanders of Israel
who offered themselves willingly among the people.

(Judges 5:6–9)

RESPONSORY

Blessed are they who observe justice, who do righteousness at all times. —**Blessed...**
Remember me, O God, when you show favor to your people; —**you, who do...**
Glory to you, Source of all Being, Eternal Word and Holy Spirit. —**Blessed...**

CANTICLE

Ant Many Samaritans from the city believed in Jesus because of the woman's testimony. They asked Jesus to stay with them.

INTERCESSIONS:

Through the intercession of Queen Esther, her people were
spared;
>—may women in power use their voices on behalf of those
>most in need.

Nations are in turmoil because of competition and greed;
>—help women in public office to bring a spirit of
>collaboration and relationship in their dealings with
>others.

The role of women has traditionally been seen as subservient;
>—grant that women may join as equal partners in
>resolving society's conflicts.

The role of government is to serve its people;
>—may women in government bring a new perspective to
>leadership and a capacity to nurture as well as govern.

Too long have the gifts of women been ignored;
>—encourage more women to seek political office as a
>means to fulfill their hopes for a better society.

PRAYER: O God, you created us both male and female, but
too often women have not been recognized or
accepted as full members of society. Grant that
their unique gifts may be used especially in the
realm of public office, that your people may be
better served. Enable those who now serve to be
faithful and effective in ways that bring our world
to greater justice for all peoples and peace among
nations. We ask this in the name of Jesus that
your will may be done and your reign be realized
here in this universe. Amen.

PSALMS

PSALMS FOR THE AGING

Psalm 21:2–8, 14

O God, your strength gives
  joy to your people;
how your saving help makes
  them glad!
You have granted them the
  desire of their hearts;
you have not refused the
  prayer of their lips.

You came to meet them with
  goodly blessings,
you have set blessings on
  their heads.
They asked you for life and
  this you have given,
length of days forever and
  ever.

Your saving help has given
  them glory.
Splendor you bestow upon
  them.
You grant your blessings to
  them forever.
You gladden them with the
  joy of your presence.

They put their trust in you;
through your steadfast love,
  they shall stand firm.
O God, we exult in your
  strength;
we shall sing and praise your
  goodness.

Lead me,
your hand shall hold me fast.

Glory to you Source of all
  Being, Eternal Word and
  Holy Spirit.

As it was in the beginning, is
  now and will be forever.
  Amen.

Psalm 71

In you, O God, I take refuge;
let me never be put to shame!
In your justice deliver and
  rescue me;
incline your ear to me and
  save me.

Be to me a rock of refuge,
a stronghold to save me,
for you are my rock and my
  stronghold.
Rescue me from the throes of
  oppression,
from the grip of injustice and
  greed.

For you, O God, are my hope,
my trust, O God, from my
  youth.
Upon you I have leaned from
  my birth;
from my mother's womb you
  claimed me.
I praise you forever and ever.

I have been a portent to
  many;
but you are my strong refuge.
My lips are filled with your
  praise,
with your glory all the day.—

Do not cast me off in old age;
forsake me not when my
strength is spent.

O God, be not far from me;
O God, make haste to help
me!
Let evil see its own
destruction,
and injustice turn on itself.

Glory to you Source of all
Being, Eternal Word and
Holy Spirit.

As it was in the beginning, is
now and will be forever.
Amen.

II

But as for me, I will always
hope
and praise you more and
more.
My lips will tell of your
justice,
of your salvation all the day,
for your goodness cannot be
numbered.

I will declare your mighty
deeds,
I will proclaim your justice,
You have taught me from my
youth,
and I proclaim your wonders
still.

Now that I am old and gray-
headed,
O God, do not forsake me,—

till I proclaim your power
to generations to come.
Your power and your justice,
O God,
reach to the highest heavens.

You have done marvelous
things,
O God, who is like you?
You who have made me see
many sore troubles
will revive me once again;
from the depths of the earth
you will raise me.
You will exalt and comfort
me again.

So I will praise you with the
harp
for your faithfulness, O God;
I will sing praises to you with
the lyre,
O Holy One of Israel.

My lips will shout for joy,
when I sing praises to you;
my soul also, which you have
redeemed.
My tongue will tell of your
justice
all the day long.

Glory to you Source of all
Being, Eternal Word and
Holy Spirit.

As it was in the beginning, is
now and will be forever.
Amen.

PSALMS IN PRAISE OF CREATION

Set A

Psalm 8

How great is your name, O
  God,
in all the earth!

You whose glory above the
  heavens
is chanted on the lips of
  babes,
have founded a defense
  against your foes,
to silence the cries of the
  rebels.

When I look at the heavens,
the work of your hands,
the moon and the stars which
  you established;
who are we that you should
  keep us in mind,
mortal flesh that you care for
  us?

Yet you have made us little
  less than God,
and crowned us with glory and
  honor.
You entrust us with the works
  of your hands,
to care for all creation.

All sheep and oxen,
and even the beasts of the
  field,
the birds of the air, and the
  fish of the sea,
whatever passes along the
  paths of the sea.

How great is your name,
  Creator God,
in all the earth!

Glory to you Source of all
  Being, Eternal Word and
  Holy Spirit.

As it was in the beginning, is
  now and will be forever.
  Amen.

Psalm 65

Praise is due to you,
O God in Zion;
and to you shall vows be
  made,
to you who hear our prayer.

To you shall all flesh come
  because of its sins.
When our offenses bear us
  down,
you forgive them all.

Blessed are we whom you
  choose and draw near,
to dwell in your courts!
We are filled with the goodness
  of your house,
your holy temple!

With wonders you deliver us,
O God of our salvation.
You are the hope of all the
  earth
and of far distant seas.

By your strength, you
  established the mountains,—

girded with might;
you still the roaring of the
   seas,
the roaring of their waves,
and the tumult of the peoples.

Those who dwell at earth's
   farthest bounds
stand in awe at your wonders;
you make the sunrise and
   sunset shout for joy.

You care for the earth, give it
   water,
you fill it with riches.
Your river in heaven brims
   over
to provide its grain.

You visit the earth and water
   it,
greatly enriching it;
you level it, soften it with
   showers,
blessing its growth.

You crown the year with your
   bounty;
Abundance flows in your path.
The pastures of the wilderness
   flow,
the hills gird themselves with
   joy,
the meadows clothe
   themselves with flocks,
the valleys deck themselves
   with grain,
they shout and sing together
   for joy.

Glory to you Source of all
   Being, Eternal Word and
   Holy Spirit.

As it was in the beginning, is
   now and will be forever.
   Amen.

Psalm 148

Praise God from the heavens,
Praise God in the heights!
Praise God, all you angels,
Praise God, you heavenly
   hosts!

Praise God, sun and moon,
Praise God, shining stars.
Praise God, highest heavens,
and the waters above the
   heavens!

Let them praise the name of
   God,
who commanded and they
   were created.
God established them forever;
fixed their bounds which will
   not pass away.

Praise God, all you on earth,
sea monsters and all deeps,
fire and hail, snow and frost,
stormy winds that obey God's
   word!

Mountains and all hills,
fruit trees and all cedars!
Beasts, wild and tame,
reptiles and birds on the wing!

All earth's rulers and peoples,
leaders and those of renown!—

Young men and women,
the old together with children!

Let us praise your name, O
God,
for your name alone is exalted;
your glory above heaven and
earth.

You exalt the strength of your
people,

you are praise for all your
saints,
for all the faithful near to you.

Glory to you Source of all
Being, Eternal Word and Holy
Spirit.

As it was in the beginning, is
now and will be forever.
Amen.

Set B

Psalm 104

Bless God, O my soul!
O God, you are very great!
You are clothed with honor
and majesty,
you cover yourself with light
as with a garment,
you have stretched out the
heavens like a tent,
you have laid the beams of
your chambers on the waters,
you make the clouds your
chariot,
you ride on the winds of the
wind,
you make the winds your
messengers—
fire and flame your ministers.

You set the earth on its
foundations,
so that it should never be
shaken.
You covered it with the deep as
with a garment;—

the waters stood above the
mountains.
At your rebuke they fled;
at the sound of your thunder
they took to flight.

The mountains rose, the
valleys sank down
to the place which you
appointed for them.
You set a bound which they
should not pass,
so that they might not again
cover the earth.

You make springs gush forth
in the valleys;
they flow between the hills,
they give drink to every beast
of the field;
the wild asses quench their
thirst.

By them the birds of the air
have their habitation;
they sing among the branches.
From your lofty abode you
water the mountains;—

the earth is satisfied with the
fruit of your work.

Glory to you Source of all
Being, Eternal Word and
Holy Spirit.

As it was in the beginning, is
now and will be forever.
Amen.

II

O God, you cause the grass to
grow for the cattle,
and plants for us to cultivate,
that we may bring forth food
from the earth,
and wine to gladden our
hearts,
oil to make our faces shine,
and bread to strengthen our
hearts.

Your trees are watered
abundantly,
the cedars of Lebanon which
you planted.
In them the birds build their
nests;
the stork has its home in the
fir trees.

The high mountains are for the
wild goats;
the rocks are a refuge for the
badgers.
You have made the moon to
mark the seasons;
the sun knows its time for
setting.

You make darkness, and it is
night,
when all the beasts of the
forests creep forth.
The young lions roar for their
prey,
seeking their food from you.
When the sun rises, they
return and lie down in their
dens.
We go forth to our work
and to our labor until the
evening.

O God, how manifold are your
works!
In wisdom you have made
them all;
the earth is full of your
creatures.

You have made the sea great
and wide,
which teems with things
innumerable,
living things both small and
great.
There go the ships,
and Leviathan which you
formed to play in it.

Glory to you Source of all
Being, Eternal Word and
Holy Spirit.

As it was in the beginning, is
now and will be forever.
Amen.

III

O God, all creation looks to
  you,
to give them their food in due
  season.
When you give to them, they
  gather it up;
when you open your hand,
they are filled with good
  things.

When you hide your face, they
  are dismayed;
when you take away their
  breath,
they die and return to their
  dust.
When you send forth your
  Spirit,
they are created;
and you renew the face of the
  earth.

May your glory, O God, endure
  for ever,
may you rejoice in all your
  works,
you, who look on the earth
  and it trembles,
who touch the mountains and
  they smoke!

I will sing to you as long as I
  live;
I will sing praise to you while I
  have being.
May my meditation be pleasing
  to you,
for I rejoice in you, O God.

Glory to you Source of all
  Being, Eternal Word and
  Holy Spirit.

As it was in the beginning, is
  now and will be forever.
  Amen.

PSALMS AT TIME OF DEATH

Set A

Psalm 23

O God, you are my shepherd;
I shall not want.
You make me to lie in green
  pastures.
You lead me to restful waters,
to restore my soul.

You guide me in paths of
  righteousness
for the sake of your name.—

Even though I walk through
  the valley of the shadow of
  death,
I fear no evil;
your crook and your staff
give me comfort.

You prepare a table before me
in the presence of my foes;
you anoint my head with oil,
my cup overflows.

Surely goodness and mercy
    shall follow me
all the days of my life.
and I shall dwell in your holy
    house
for ever and ever.

Glory to you Source of all
    Being, Eternal Word and
    Holy Spirit.

As it was in the beginning, is
    now and will be forever.
    Amen.

Psalm 25

To you, O God, I lift up my
    soul.
In you, I trust, let me not be
    put to shame;
let not the wicked exult over
    me.
Those who wait on you shall
    not be put to shame;
but only those who wantonly
    break faith.

Make me know your ways, O
    God;
Teach me your paths.
Lead me in your truth, and
    teach me,
for you are God, my savior.
For you I wait all the day long.

Remember your mercy, O God,
and your steadfast love,
which you have given from of
    old.
Remember not the sins of my
    youth,—

or my transgressions;
But in your goodness,
    remember me
according to your steadfast
    love!

You, O God, are good and
    upright.
You instruct sinners in your
    way.
You lead the humble in the
    right path;
and teach your way to the
    poor.

All your ways are loving and
    constant
for those who keep your
    covenant and your decrees.
For your name's sake, O God,
pardon my guilt, for it is great.

Glory to you Source of all
    Being, Eternal Word and
    Holy Spirit.

As it was in the beginning, is
    now and will be forever.
    Amen.

Psalm 27

O God, you are my light and
    my help;
whom shall I fear?
You are the stronghold of my
    life;
before whom shall I be afraid?

When evildoers assail me
uttering slanders against me,
it is they, my enemies and
    foes,—

who shall stumble and fall.

Though an army encamp
  against me
my heart shall not fear.
Though war break out against
  me
yet will I trust.

One thing I have asked of you,
for this will I seek,
that I may dwell in your holy
  house
all the days of my life,
to behold the beauty of your
  countenance
and the holiness of your
  temple.

In your shelter you will hide
  me
in the day of trouble;—

you will conceal me under the
  cover of your tent,
you will set me high upon a
  rock.

And now my head shall be
  raised
above my foes who surround
  me
and I will offer in your tent
sacrifices with songs of joy.
I will sing and make music to
  my God.

Glory to you Source of all
  Being, Eternal Word and
  Holy Spirit.

As it was in the beginning, is
  now and will be forever.
  Amen.

Set B

Psalm 42:1–5

Like the deer that yearns
for flowing streams,
so my soul is longing
for you my God.

My soul is thirsting for God,
the living God.
When shall I come and see,
the face of God?

My tears have become my
  food,
by night and day,
while I hear it said all day,
"Where is your God?"

These things will I remember
as I pour out my soul:
how I led the throng,
to the house of God,
with shouts of gladness and
  songs of thanksgiving,
the multitude keeping
  festival.

Why are you cast down, my
  soul,
why disquieted within me?
Hope in God; I will again
  praise you,
my help and my God.

Glory to you Source of all
Being, Eternal Word and
Holy Spirit.

As it was in the beginning, is
now and will be forever.
Amen.

Glory to you Source of all
Being, Eternal Word and
Holy Spirit.

As it was in the beginning, is
now and will be forever.
Amen.

Psalm 43

Defend me, O God, and plead
  my cause
against a godless nation.
From the deceitful and the
  unjust
rescue me, O God.

For in you I take refuge;
why have you cast me off?
Why do I go mourning
because of oppression?

O send out your light and
  your truth;
let these be my guide.
Let them bring me to your
  holy hill
and to your dwelling place.

Then I will go to the altar of
  God,
to God, my exceeding joy;
and I will praise you with the
  lyre,
O God, my God.

Why are you cast down, my
  soul,
why groan within me?
Hope in God: I shall again
  praise
my savior and my God.

Revelation 11:17–18; 12:10b–12a

We give thanks to you, God
  Almighty,
who is and who was,
you have assumed your great
  power,
you have begun your reign.

The nations raged, but your
  wrath came,
and the time for the dead to
  be judged,
for rewarding your servants,
  the prophets and saints,
and those who revere your
  name,
the great and small alike.

Now the salvation, the power,
  and the reign have come,
of God and of the Christ,
for the accusers of our loved
  ones have been thrown
  down,
who accuse them day and
  night.

They have been conquered by
  the blood of the Lamb,
and by the word of their
  testimony,—

for love of life did not deter
them from death.
Rejoice then, O heaven,
and you that dwell therein!

Glory to you Source of all
Being, Eternal Word and
Holy Spirit.

As it was in the beginning, is
now and will be forever.
Amen.

PSALMS IN TIMES OF DISTRESS

Set A

Psalm 55:1–19, 22–24

O God, give ear to my
prayer;
hide not from my
supplication!
Attend to me and answer
me;
I am overcome by my
troubles.

I am distraught by the lure
of corruption,
at oppression caused by
wickedness.
The evil that brings trouble
upon me,
and whose anger weighs on
my soul.

My heart is in anguish
within me,
the terrors of death fall upon
me.
Fear and trembling come
upon me,
and horror overwhelms me.

O that I had wings like a
dove!—

I would fly away and be at
rest;
indeed, I would wander afar.
I would take refuge in the
wilderness,
I would haste to find me a
shelter
from the raging wind and
tempest.

Overthrow this oppression,
O God,
confuse all that seeks to
destroy,
For I see violence and strife
all around me.
Day and night it patrols our
cities;
They are full of wickedness
and evil,
ruin is in their midst;
oppression and fraud do not
depart
from their marketplaces.

Glory to you Source of all
Being, Eternal Word and
Holy Spirit.

As it was in the beginning, is
now and will be forever.
Amen.

II

It is not our enemies who
cause this;
then I might bear it;
it is not our foes who
oppress,
I might hide from them.

But it is ourselves, our
companions,
our familiar and intimate
friends.
We used to speak together of
justice;
We walked together in
companionship
in the ways of our God.

I will call out to you, O God,
and you will save me.
Evening, morning and at
noon
I utter complaint and
lament;
you will hear my voice.

You will deliver my soul in
safety
in the attack waged all
around;
for many things can bring
me down,
but you will hear my cry.

You will give ear, and
chastise us,
you, who reign from of old;—

because we have not kept
your law,
and have not revered you.

Cast your burdens on our
God,
and you will be supported.
Never will God permit
the just ones to falter.

But you, O God, will bring
down
to the pit of the grave,
all that is wicked and evil,
that oppresses the poor and
the needy.

O God, we will trust in you.

Glory to you Source of all
Being, Eternal Word and
Holy Spirit.

As it was in the beginning, is
now and will be forever.
Amen.

Psalm 130

Out of the depths I cry to
you,
O God, hear my voice!
Let your ears be attentive
to the voice of my
supplication.

If you should mark our
iniquities,
O God, who could stand?
But with you is found
forgiveness:
for this we revere you.

My soul waits for you,
in your word I hope;
my soul waits for you
more than those who watch
  for daybreak.

Let Israel hope in you!
For with you there is love,
  and fullness of
  redemption.—

And you will redeem Israel
from all its iniquities.

Glory to you Source of all
  Being, Eternal Word and
  Holy Spirit.

As it was in the beginning, is
  now and will be forever.
  Amen.

Set B

Psalm 28:1–3, 6–9

To you, O God, I call,
my rock, be not deaf to me.
If you turn your ear away
  from me,
I become like those in the
  grave.

Hear the voice of my
  pleading
as I cry to you for help,
as I lift up my hands in
  prayer
to your holy sanctuary.

Do not take me away with
  the wicked,
with those who are workers
  of evil,
who speak peace with their
  neighbors,
while evil is in their hearts.

I bless you, for you have
  heard
the voice of my supplication.
You are my strength and my
  shield;
in you my heart trusts.—

I am helped, and my heart
  exults,
with my song I give you
  thanks.

You are the strength of your
  people,
you are the refuge of your
  anointed.
Save your people; and bless
  your heritage;
be their shepherd and carry
  them forever.

Glory to you Source of all
  Being, Eternal Word and
  Holy Spirit.

As it was in the beginning, is
  now and will be forever.
  Amen.

Psalm 56:1–7b, 9–14

Be gracious to me, O God,
some there are who crush
  me;
they trample upon me all
  day long,—

for many fight proudly
against me.

When I am afraid,
I put my trust in you.
In you, whose word I praise,
In you I trust without fear.
What can mortal flesh do to
me?

All day long they injure my
cause,
all their thoughts are for evil.
They band together, they
lurk,
they watch my steps.

You have kept count of my
wanderings;
you have kept a record of my
tears!
Are they not written in your
book?
Then my foes will be turned
back
in the day when I call to you.

This I know, that God is with
me.
In God, whose word I praise,
in the Holy One, whose word
I praise,
in God I trust without a fear.
What can mortal flesh do to
me?

My vows to you I will make,
O God.
I will render you thanks.
For you delivered my soul
from death,
my feet from falling,—

that I may walk before you
in the light of life.

Glory to you Source of all
Being, Eternal Word and
Holy Spirit.

As it was in the beginning, is
now and will be forever.
Amen.

Psalm 57

Have mercy on me, have
mercy,
for in you my soul takes
refuge.
In the shadow of your wings
I take refuge
till the storms of destruction
pass by.

I cry to God the Most High,
to God who has always been
my help.
May you send from heaven
and save me
and shame those who
trample upon me.
O God, send down your
truth and your love.

My soul lies down among
lions,
who greedily devour the
peoples of the earth.
Their teeth are spears and
arrows,
their tongue a sharpened
sword.

Be exalted, O God, above the
heavens;—

Be exalted, O God, above the
heavens;—
let your glory be over all the
earth!

They laid a snare for my
steps,
my soul was bowed down.
They dug a pit in my path
but they fell in it themselves.

My heart is steadfast, O
God,
my heart is steadfast.
I will sing and make melody!
Awake, my soul,
awake, lyre and harp!
I will awake the dawn!

I will give thanks to you
among the peoples,

I will praise you among the
nations,
for your love reaches to the
heavens,
your faithfulness to the
skies.

Be exalted, O God, above the
heavens!
let your glory be over the
earth!

Glory to you Source of all
Being, Eternal Word and
Holy Spirit.

As it was in the beginning, is
now and will be forever.
Amen.

PSALMS FOR EVERY DAY

Set A

Psalm 84

How lovely is your dwelling
place,
O my God!

My soul longs and yearns
for the courts of the Most
High;
my heart and lips sing for
joy
to you the living God.

Even the sparrow finds a
home,
and the swallow a nest for
its brood,

where it may lay its young,
at your altars, O my God!

Blessed are those who dwell
in your house,
forever singing your praise!
Blessed are those whose
strength you are,
in whose hearts are the
roads to Zion.

As they go through the Bitter
Valley,
they make it a place of
springs;

O God, hear my prayer;
give ear, O God of our
  mothers!
Look upon our shield, O
  God;
look on the face of your
  anointed!

For one day in your courts is
  better
than a thousand anywhere
  else.
I would rather stand at your
  threshold
than dwell in the tents of
  wickedness.

For you are a sun and a
  shield;
you bestow favor and honor.
No good do you withhold
from those who walk
  uprightly.

O God, my God!
Blessed are those who trust
  in you!

Glory to you Source of all
  Being, Eternal Word and
  Holy Spirit.

As it was in the beginning, is
  now and will be forever.
  Amen.

Psalm 16

Preserve me, O God, for in
  you I take refuge.
I say to you: "You are my
  God;—

I have no good apart from
  you."
All my delight is in your
  saints;
the faithful who dwell in
  your land.

Those who choose other gods
  increase their sorrows;
their offerings of blood I will
  not pour out
or take their names upon my
  lips.

You are my portion and my
  cup;
you are my fortune, my
  prize.
The lines have fallen for me
  in pleasant places;
I have been given a welcome
  heritage.

I will bless you who give me
  counsel;
in the night my heart
  instructs me.
I keep you always before me;
because you are near, I shall
  stand firm.

Therefore my heart is glad,
  and my soul rejoices;
even my body rests securely.
For you do not give me up to
  death,
or let your faithful see the
  grave.

You will show me the path of
  life;—

in your presence there is
fullness of joy,
in your hands, happiness
forever.

Glory to you Source of all
Being, Eternal Word and
Holy Spirit.

As it was in the beginning, is
now and will be forever.
Amen.

Psalm 113

We your servants, praise
you!
Praise your holy name!
Blessed be your name, O
God,
from now and forevermore!
From the rising of the sun to
its setting
your name is to be praised!

You are high above all
nations,
and your glory above the
heavens!—

Who is like unto you, O God,
who is seated upon the
heights,
who looks far down upon us,
upon the heavens and the
earth?

You raise the poor from the
dust,
lift the needy from the ash
heap,
to set them in the company
of rulers,
with the rulers of your
people.
To the barren, you give a
home,
and gladden their hearts
with children.

Glory to you Source of all
Being, Eternal Word and
Holy Spirit.

As it was in the beginning, is
now and will be forever.
Amen.

Set B

Psalm 121

I lift up my eyes to the hills.
From whence comes my
help?
My help comes from you, O
God,
who made heaven and earth.

You will not let my foot
stumble,—

you, who preserve me, will
not sleep.
Behold, you who keep Israel
will neither slumber nor
sleep.

You, O God, are our keeper;
you are our shade.
The sun shall not smite us
by day,
nor the moon by night.

You will guard us from all
  evil;
you will preserve our lives.
You will protect our goings
  and comings
both now and forever.

Glory to you Source of all
  Being, Eternal Word and
  Holy Spirit.

As it was in the beginning, is
now and will be forever.
Amen.

Isaiah 12:1-6

I will give thanks to you, O
  God;
for though you were angry
  with me,
your anger turned away,
and you did comfort me.

Behold, you are my savior;
I will trust, and will not be
  afraid;
you are my strength and my
  song,
you have become my
  salvation.

With joy we will draw water
  from the wells of salvation.
We will say on that day:
"We give you thanks and call
  upon your name;
make known your deeds
  among the nations,
proclaim how exalted is your
  name.

"We sing our praise to you,
for all your glorious deeds;
let this be known in all the
  earth."
Shout, and sing for joy,
  O people of Zion,
for great in your midst
is the Holy One of Israel!

Glory to you Source of all
  Being, Eternal Word and
  Holy Spirit.

As it was in the beginning, is
now and will be forever.
Amen.

Psalm 67

O God, be gracious to us
  and bless us,
and make your face shine
  upon us.
That your ways be known
  upon earth,
your saving power among all
  nations.
Let the peoples praise you, O
  God;
let all the peoples praise
  you.

Let the nations be glad and
  sing for joy,
for you judge the peoples
  with equity
and guide the nations on
  earth.
Let the peoples praise you, O
  God;—

for you judge the peoples
with equity
and guide the nations on
earth.
Let the peoples praise you, O
God;—
let all the peoples praise
you.

The earth has yielded its
increase;

God, our God, has blessed
us.
You, indeed, have blessed
us;—
let all the earth revere you!

Glory to you Source of all
Being, Eternal Word and
Holy Spirit.

As it was in the beginning, is
now and will be forever.
Amen.

PSALMS FOR FEASTS

Set A

Psalm 63:1–9

O God, you are my God, I
long for you;
My body seeks for you
as in a dry and weary land
without water.
So I have looked upon you in
the sanctuary,
beholding your power and
your glory.

For your constant love is
better than life,
my lips will sing your
praises.
So I will bless you as long as
I live;
I will lift up my hands and
call on your name.

My soul feasts on you and
my mouth praises you,
as I think of you upon my
bed,

and meditate on you in the
watches of the night;
for you have been my help,—
In the shadow of your wings
I sing for joy.
My soul clings to you; your
right hand upholds me.

Glory to you Source of all
Being, Eternal Word and
Holy Spirit.

As it was in the beginning, is
now and will be forever.
Amen.

Cant.: Daniel 3:57–88, 56

All you works of God, praise
our God.
Praise and exalt God above
all forever.
All you angels, sing God's
praise,

Every shower and dew,
   praise our God.
Give praise all you winds.
Praise our God, you fire and
   heat,
cold and chill, dew and rain.
Frost and chill, praise our
   God.
Praise God, ice and snow.
Nights and days, sing hymns
   of praise,
light and darkness,
lightnings and clouds.

Let all the earth bless our
   God.
Praise and exalt God above
   all forever.
Let all that grows from the
   earth give praise
together with mountains and
   hills.
Give praise, you springs,
you seas and rivers,
dolphins and all water
   creatures.
Let birds of the air,
beasts, wild and tame,
together with all living
   peoples,
praise and exalt God above
   all forever.

O Israel, praise our God.
Praise and exalt God above
   all forever.
Give praise, you priests,
servants of the Most High,
spirits and souls of the just.
Holy ones of humble heart,—

sing your hymns of praise.
Hannaniah, Azariah,
   Mishael, praise our God.
Praise and exalt God above
   all forever.

Let us bless our God, Holy
   Mystery,
Source of All Being, Word
   and Spirit.
Let us praise and exalt God
   above all forever.
Blessed are you, O God, in
   the firmament of heaven.
Praiseworthy and glorious
   and exalted above all
   forever.

Psalm 149

Sing a new song to our God,
Give praise in the assembly
   of the faithful.
Let Israel be glad in its
   maker,
let Zion's heirs exult in the
   Most High.
Let them praise God's name
   with dancing,
and make music with
   timbrel and harp.

For you take delight in your
   people, O God.
You adorn the humble with
   victory.
Let the faithful exult in their
   glory,
in their rest, let them sing
   for joy.

Let the praises of God be on
  their lips
and two-edged swords in
  their hands,

to wreak vengeance on all
  that is wicked,
and chastisement on all
  injustice;
to bind what is evil in chains
and oppression in fetters of
  iron;—

to carry out the sentence
  preordained;
this is glory for all God's
  faithful ones.

Glory to you Source of all
  Being, Eternal Word and
  Holy Spirit.

As it was in the beginning, is
  now and will be forever.
  Amen.

Set B

Psalm 110:1–5, 7

God's revelation to the
  Anointed One:
"Sit at my side:
till I put injustice beneath
  your feet."

God will send forth from
  Zion
your scepter of power:
rule in the midst of your
  foes.

Your people will give
  themselves freely
on the day you lead your
  host upon the holy
  mountain.
From the womb of the
  morning
your youth will come like
  dew.

God has sworn an oath that
  will not be changed.
"You are a priest forever,—

after the order of
  Melchizedek."

The Anointed standing at
  your right hand
will shatter rulers on the day
  of wrath.

Drinking from your streams
  by the wayside
shall the Chosen One be
  refreshed.

Glory to you Source of all
  Being, Eternal Word and
  Holy Spirit.

As it was in the beginning, is
  now and will be forever.
  Amen.

Psalm 114

When Israel went forth from
  Egypt,
Jacob's heirs from an alien
  people,—

Judah became God's
sanctuary,
Israel, the dominion of the
Most High.

The sea looked and fled,
Jordan turned back on its
course.
The mountains skipped like
rams,
the hills like yearling lambs.

What ails you, O sea, that
you flee?
O Jordan, that you turn
back?
Mountains, that you skip
like rams,
hills, like yearling lambs?

Tremble, O earth, at the
presence of God,
at the presence of the God of
your ancestors,
who turns the rock into a
pool,
the flint into a spring of
water.

Glory to you Source of all
Being, Eternal Word and
Holy Spirit.

As it was in the beginning, is
now and will be forever.
Amen.

Canticle: Revelation 19:1, 5–7

Salvation, glory, and power
belong to you,
your judgments are honest
and true.

All of us, your servants, sing
praise to you,
we worship you reverently,
both great and small.

You, our almighty God, are
Creator of heaven and
earth.
Let us rejoice and exult, and
give you glory.

The wedding feast of the
Lamb has begun,
And the bride has made
herself ready.

Glory to you Source of all
Being, Eternal Word and
Holy Spirit.

As it was in the beginning, is
now and will be forever.
Amen.

PSALMS FOR FEASTS OF OUR LADY

Psalm 113

We your servants, praise you!
Praise your holy name!
Blessed be your name, O God,
from now and for evermore!
From the rising of the sun to
its setting
your name is to be praised!

You are high above all nations,
and your glory above the
heavens!
Who is like unto you, O God,
who is seated upon the
heights,
who looks far down upon us,
upon the heavens and the
earth?

You raise the poor from the
dust,
lift the needy from the ash
heap,
to set them in the company of
rulers,
with the rulers of your people.
To the barren, you give a
home,
and gladden their hearts with
children.

Glory to you Source of all
Being, Eternal Word and
Holy Spirit.

As it was in the beginning, is
now and will be forever.
Amen.

Psalm 147:12–20

O praise the Most High,
Jerusalem!
Praise your God, O Zion!

For God strengthens the bars
of your gates,
blessing your children within
you,
establishing peace in your
borders,
feeding you with the finest of
wheat.

You send out your word to the
earth;
your command runs swiftly,
giving snow like wool,
scattering hoarfrost like ashes.

You cast forth your ice like
crumbs;
who can stand before your
cold?
You send forth your word, and
melt them;
you make the wind blow, and
the waters flow.

You make your word known to
your people,
your statutes and decrees to
Israel.
You have not dealt thus with
any other nation;
you have not taught them your
decrees.

Glory to you Source of all
  Being, Eternal Word and
  Holy Spirit.

As it was in the beginning, is
  now and will be forever.
  Amen.

Ephesians 1:3–10

Praised be the God of our Lord
  Jesus Christ
who has blessed us in Christ
with every spiritual blessing in
  the heavens.

God chose us in him
before the foundation of the
  world,
that we should be holy
and blameless in God's sight.

We have been predestined
to be God's children through
  Jesus Christ,
such was the purpose of God's
  will,
that all might praise the
  glorious favor
bestowed on us in Christ.

In Christ and through his
  blood,
we have redemption,
the forgiveness of our sins,
according to the riches of
  God's grace
lavished upon us.

For God has made known to
  us
in all wisdom and insight,
the mystery of the plan set
  forth in Christ.

A plan to be carried out in
  Christ,
in the fullness of time,
to unite all things in Christ,
things in heaven and things on
  earth.

Glory to you Source of all
  Being, Eternal Word and
  Holy Spirit.

As it was in the beginning, is
  now and will be forever.
  Amen.

PSALMS FOR MOTHERS

Psalm 139:1-18, 23-24

O God, you have searched me
and you know me,
you know when I sit and when
I stand;
you discern my thoughts from
afar.
You mark when I walk or lie
down,
with all my ways you are
acquainted.

Before a word is on my tongue,
behold, O God, you know the
whole of it.
Behind and before you besiege
me,
you lay your hand upon me.
Such knowledge is too
wonderful for me;
too high, beyond my reach.

O where can I go from your
spirit,
or where can I flee from your
presence?
If I climb to heaven, you are
there!
If I lie in the grave, you are
there!

If I take the wings of the
morning
and dwell in the depths of the
sea,
even there your hand shall
lead me,
your hand shall hold me fast.

If I say: "Let darkness cover
me,
and the light around me be
night,"
even darkness is not dark to
you
and the night is as bright as
the day;
for darkness is as light to you.

Glory to you Source of all
Being, Eternal Word and
Holy Spirit.

As it was in the beginning, is
now and will be forever.
Amen.

II

For it was you who formed my
inmost parts,
knit me together in my
mother's womb.
I praise you for the wonder of
my being,
for the wonder of all your
works.

Already you knew me well;
my body was not hidden from
you,
when I was being made in
secret
and molded in the depths of
the earth.

Your eyes beheld my unformed
substance;—

in your book they all were
written,
the days that you had formed
for me
when none of them yet were.

How precious to me are your
thoughts!
How vast the sum of them!
If I count them, they are more
than the sand.
When I awake, I am still with
you.

Search me, O God, and know
my heart!
O test me and know my
thoughts!
See that I follow not the wrong
way
and lead me in the way of life
eternal.

Glory to you Source of all
Being, Eternal Word and
Holy Spirit.

As it was in the beginning, is
now and will be forever.
Amen.

Psalm 127

If God does not build the
house,—

its builders labor in vain.
If God does not watch over the
city,
in vain is the vigil kept.

It is vain to rise up early
and go late to rest,
eating the bread of anxious
toil:
for you, O God, give sleep to
your beloved.

Truly children are a gift from
God,
the fruit of the womb, a
blessing.
Like arrows in the hand of a
warrior
are the children of one's youth.

Happy the couple who have
their quiver full of them!
They shall not be put to shame
when they encounter distress.

Glory to you Source of all
Being, Eternal Word and
Holy Spirit.

As it was in the beginning, is
now and will be forever.
Amen.

PSALMS FOR SOCIAL JUSTICE

Set A

Psalm 94

God of justice,
just God, appear!—

Judge of the earth, arise,
render injustice its deserts!
How long, O God, shall
oppression,—

how long shall oppression
exult?

They bluster with arrogant
speech,
they boast, all the evildoers.
They crush your people, O
God,
they afflict the ones you have
chosen.
They kill the helpless and the
poor,
and murder the parentless
child.
They say: "God does not see;
their God pays no heed!"

Understand, O dullest of
people!
Fools, when will you be wise?
Can God who made the ear,
not hear?
The one who formed the eye,
not see?
Will God who chastens
nations, not punish?
God who imparts knowledge
knows our thoughts,
knows they are no more than
a breath.

Glory to you Source of all
Being, Eternal Word and
Holy Spirit.

As it was in the beginning, is
now and will be forever.
Amen.

II

Happy are those whom you
chasten,
whom you teach by means of
your law
to give them respite from days
of trouble,
until oppression is no more.
You will not abandon your
people;
you will not forsake your
heritage;
for justice will return to the
righteous,
and the upright in heart will
follow it.

Who will rise against
oppression?
Who will stand against
injustice?
If you had not been my help,
I would soon dwell in the land
of silence.

When I think: "My foot is
slipping,"
your steadfast love upholds
me.
When the cares of my heart
are many,
your consolations cheer my
soul.

Can unjust rulers be your
friends,
who do injustice under cover
of law?
They attack the life of the
helpless,—

and condemn the innocent to death.

But you have become my stronghold,
my God, the rock of my refuge.
Injustice will turn on itself,
and evil will destroy evil.

Glory to you Source of all Being, Eternal Word and Holy Spirit.

As it was in the beginning, is now and will be forever. Amen.

Psalm 43

Defend me, O God, and plead my cause
against a godless nation.
From the deceitful and the unjust
rescue me, O God.

For in you I take refuge;
why have you cast me off?
Why do I go mourning
because of oppression?

O send out your light and your truth;
let these be my guide.
Let them bring me to your holy hill
and to your dwelling place.

Then I will go to the altar of God,
to God, my exceeding joy;
and I will praise you with the lyre,
O God, my God.

Why are you cast down, my soul,
why groan within me?
Hope in God; I shall again praise
my savior and my God.

Glory to you Source of all Being, Eternal Word and Holy Spirit.

As it was in the beginning, is now and will be forever. Amen.

Set B

Jeremiah 14:17-21

Let my eyes stream with tears
night and day, without rest,
for the virgin daughter of my people
is smitten with a great wound,
with a very grievous blow.

If I walk out into the field,
behold, those slain by the sword!
If I enter the city,
behold, the diseases of famine!
Both the prophet and the priest—

ply their trade throughout
  the land,
ignorant of their doings.

Have you utterly rejected
  Judah?
Is Zion loathsome to you?
Why have you smitten us
so that there is no healing?

We looked for peace to no
  avail;
for a time of healing,
but terror comes instead.
We acknowledge our
  sinfulness,
and the guilt of our
  ancestors,
for we have sinned against
  you.

Spurn us not for your name's
  sake;
do not dishonor your glorious
  throne;
remember your covenant
  with us,
and break it not.

Glory to you Source of all
  Being, Eternal Word and
  Holy Spirit.

As it was in the beginning, is
  now and will be forever.
  Amen.

Psalm 72

Give justice to your Anointed,
  O God,
and righteousness to those
  Chosen!—

That your people may be
  judged in righteousness,
and your poor with justice.

Let the mountains bring forth
  peace for the people,
and the hills, justice!
May your Anointed
defend the cause of the poor,
give deliverance to the needy,
and punish the oppressor!

May your Anointed endure
  like the sun,
and as long as the moon,
  through all ages,
like rain that falls on the
  mown grass,
like showers that water the
  earth.

In that day justice shall
  flourish
and peace till the moon be no
  more!
Your Anointed shall rule from
  sea to sea,
from the river to the ends of
  the earth!

Glory to you Source of all
  Being, Eternal Word and
  Holy Spirit.

As it was in the beginning, is
  now and will be forever.
  Amen.

II

The Anointed delivers the
  needy when they call,—

the poor and those who are
  helpless.
Having pity on the weak and
  the needy,
saving the lives of the poor.

From oppression and
  violence they are redeemed;
and precious is their blood.
Long may your Chosen One
  live,
may gold of Sheba be given
to the one you have anointed,
and prayers be made without
  ceasing,
and blessings all the day!

May there be abundance of
  grain in the land,
waving on the tops of the
  mountains;
may its fruit be like Lebanon;
may people flourish in the
  cities
like the grass in the field!

May the name of your
  Anointed endure forever,
and continue as long as the
  sun!
Every tribe shall be blessed
  in the one you have chosen,
all nations bless your name.

Blessed be God, God of
  Israel,
who alone does wondrous
  things.
Blessed be your name
  forever;
may your glory fill the earth.
Amen! Amen!

Glory to you Source of all
  Being, Eternal Word and
  Holy Spirit.

As it was in the beginning, is
  now and will be forever.
  Amen.

WOMEN
OF
INSPIRATION

January 4
ST. ELIZABETH ANN BAYLEY SETON

Elizabeth Seton, widow, mother, and convert to Roman Catholicism, is the first native born American saint. She founded the American Sisters of Charity, established the first free Catholic day school, and opened the first Catholic orphanage. She was known for her works of mercy and charity. Elizabeth Seton died January 4, 1821.

MORNING/EVENING PRAYER

(Psalms for Feasts, p. 75, or p. 77)

Ant 1 God has done great things for me; may God be forever praised, alleluia.

Ant 2 The valiant woman is a pearl of great price—all generations will call her blessed, alleluia.

Ant 3 What you have done for the least of my sisters and brothers, you have done for me, alleluia.

REFLECTION/SHARING

...You know I am as a mother encompassed by many children of different dispositions, not all equally amiable or congenial; but bound to love, instruct and provide for the happiness of all, to give the example of cheerfulness, peace, resignation, and consider individuals more as proceeding from the same origin and tending to the same end than in the different shades of merit or demerit.*

RESPONSORY

Those who sow in tears shall reap with shouts of joy. —**Those**...
She who goes forth weeping; —**shall**...
Glory to you, Source of all Being, Eternal Word and Holy Spirit.
   —**Those**...

CANTICLE

Ant Many waters cannot quench love, neither can floods drown it.

INTERCESSIONS:

O God, you raised up Elizabeth Seton to be an inspiration for many. In thanksgiving for the gift of her life, we pray:
Blessed be God forever!

Elizabeth Seton was widowed at an early age;
   —may all who sorrow and are lonely be comforted.
She was the mother of five children;
   —grant those entrusted with the rearing of children the wisdom to guide them.
Through the intercession of Elizabeth Seton, a convert to Catholicism;
   —may we come to more understanding of and appreciation for our differences in our efforts to live the gospel.
You inspired her to found the Sisters of Charity;
   —help us to be faithful to our religious commitment, that we may be transformed into Christ.
You filled her with zeal for the education of youth;
   —guide all teachers and educators to enable students to grow in knowledge and to become good citizens of the earth and heirs of heaven.

PRAYER: O God, we give you thanks for the life of Elizabeth Seton. May the values she cherished be realized in our world that all may enjoy a better quality of life. May the holiness of her life inspire us to serve you and work only for your glory. Bless all the Sisters of Charity that they may faithfully continue the work she began. We ask this in the name of Jesus. Amen.

* Excerpts from her writings.

January 12
ST. MARGUERITE BOURGEOYS*

St. Marguerite Bourgeoys left her native France in 1653 for the newly founded colony of Ville Marie, the present-day city of Montreal in Canada, where she played a vital role in the lives of young couples and their families. In 1658 she opened the first school, a renovated stone stable, for the children of the native people and the French colonists, and soon became lovingly known as the "Mother of the Colony." That same year she founded the Congregation of Notre Dame, the first uncloistered community of women in the New World. Inspired by the mystery of Mary's Visitation to Elizabeth and of her presence among the apostles in the first Christian community, Marguerite proclaimed by her life that fidelity to a dream and a vision is costly. Canonized in 1982, she stands as an inspiration and a challenge to women disciples in our contemporary Church and world.

MORNING/EVENING PRAYER

(Psalms for Feasts, p. 75, or p. 77)

Ant 1 All that I have ever desired is that the great precept of the love of God and neighbor be written in every heart.

Ant 2 Charcoal that is fired all the way to the center is not extinguished, but is consumed.

Ant 3 It is only the love of the lover that penetrates the heart of God.

REFLECTION/SHARING

...We read that in God the first Christians had only one heart and one soul; that they possessed nothing individually,...that all their property was held in common among them.... So it was that the Blessed Virgin who was, after the death of her Son, the only superior of this first community, as she is ours today, formed these happy Christians. In the same way, we ought to be perfectly united in the Congregation. Without this union, we cannot flatter ourselves that we are living under the auspices of this good Mother.... God is not satisfied if we preserve the love we owe our neighbor; we must preserve our neighbor in the love she ought to have for us.**

RESPONSORY

All that I have ever desired is that the great precept of the love of God above all things be written in every heart. —**All that**...
And of the love of neighbor as oneself; —**be written**...
Glory to you, Source of all Being, Eternal Word and Holy Spirit.
   —**All that**...

CANTICLE

Ant The woman said, "Go, I will not abandon you," and I knew it was the Blessed Virgin.

INTERCESSIONS:

Spirit of the living God, confirm the awareness of your presence
alive and active in us and among us as we celebrate this feast
of Marguerite Bourgeoys. Let us pray:
We praise you for the gift of her life.

You gifted Marguerite with a love for your Church and a desire
that it be a faithful witness of Christ among your people;
> —may you enable us to respond with love and compassion to
> the special needs of the Church in our time.

You inspired her to found the Sisters of the Congregation of
Notre Dame to live and proclaim the gospel as educators;
> —guide all teachers and educators as they enable others to
> grow in knowledge, wisdom, and gospel values.

You gifted her with a special love for those who are needy and
poor;
> —enable us to reflect her spirit in our presence and service
> among those who are needy and poor in our time.

You filled her with a desire to imitate the life that Mary led
throughout her time on earth;
> —may we be graced, like Mary, to live in openness to the
> Spirit and to respond with courage to your call in our daily
> lives.

PRAYER: O God, you called Marguerite Bourgeoys to leave her
country to extend your realm by educating your
people in the Christian way of life. Grant that,
inspired by her example and assisted by her prayer,
we may proclaim by our word and action the
presence of Jesus to all who seek paths that lead to
you. Bless especially the Sisters of the Congregation
of Notre Dame, that they may be given the grace to
live faithfully in the spirit and vision of Marguerite
Bourgeoys and to be transformed by it. We ask you
this in the name of Jesus. Amen.

* Composed by the Sisters of the Congregation of Notre Dame.
** Excerpts from her writings

January 23
MARY WARD

Mary Ward was born in England in 1585; she died there in 1645. The years between took her on a journey of faith to found and shape a new kind of religious life for women. In order to be better adapted to the needs of the times, it would be free of enclosure and governed by women. Gropingly, tentatively, painfully, she began the loneliness of the long journey that led to the fulfillment of her own prophecy that women would share actively in the church's ministry. Her companions today are known as members of the Institute of the Blessed Virgin Mary. Mary Ward died January 30, 1645.

MORNING/EVENING PRAYER

(Psalms for Feasts, p. 75, or p. 77)

Ant 1 Blessed are you when people revile you and say all manner of evil against you; your reward shall be great.

Ant 2 My God, cast us not away from your face, and take not your Spirit from us.

Ant 3 You have broken my bonds; so I will offer to you a sacrifice of praise.

REFLECTION/SHARING

I think, dear child, the trouble and the long loneliness you hear me speak of is not far from me, which whensoever it is, happy success will follow.... The pain is great, but very endurable, because [the One] who lays on the burden also carries it.*

Our greatness and strength consist not in the favor of princes and great personages, but in this: we have free and open access to God from whom all greatness and strength come.*

RESPONSORY

Suffering without sin is no burden; into your hands I commend my spirit.* —Suffering...
Show me your mercy and grant me your salvation; —into your...
Glory to you, Source of all Being, Eternal Word and Holy Spirit.
   —Suffering...

CANTICLE

Ant God will assist and help you, it is no matter the who but the what; and when God shall enable me to return, I will serve you.*

INTERCESSIONS:

Christ Jesus, you were rejected by your own but your love never failed. In hope we pray:
Shelter us in the shadow of your wings.

O God, your daughter Mary was labeled as "heretic, schismatic, rebel to Holy Church," and her congregation was suppressed;
—grant courage to those misunderstood or misjudged by ecclesiastical or civil authorities.

O God, in spite of failure and exile, Mary accepted all with patience and a sense of humor;
—grant us hearts that are humble and help us to not take ourselves too seriously.

Imprisoned, Mary was refused the sacraments even when she was thought to be dying;
—comfort all who are unjustly imprisoned and give them hope.

O God, you gifted Mary with vision and courage;
—support all those whose vision and gifts further the work of bringing this world to fullness of life especially in their times of trial.

PRAYER: O God, purify our hearts and give us courage to work for the coming of your reign in our hearts. Knowing that the work we do is yours to accomplish, let us not be discouraged by lack of results. We thank you for all those who have faithfully persevered in spite of adversity and ask them to intercede for us. Grant this through Jesus who is our Way, our Truth, and our Life. Amen.

* Excerpts from her writings.

January 27
ST. ANGELA MERICI

Angela Merici, born in Italy in the latter part of the fifteenth century, dedicated herself to catechetical and religious works as a young woman. Going to Brescia in her forties, she sought to support young girls in leading a Christian life in a decadent society. In her early sixties, she founded the Ursulines, a group of women who originally lived in their own homes, served the needy, and met monthly for mutual support. Angela sought to transform society through the renewal of family life and Christian education. She died in 1540.

MORNING/EVENING PRAYER

(Psalms for Feasts, p. 75, or p. 77)

Ant 1 Have hope and firm faith that God will help you in all things.*

Ant 2 Blessed are those who sincerely take up the work of serving God's people.

Ant 3 Let your first refuge always be at the feet of Jesus Christ.*

REFLECTION/SHARING

In [Angela's] reckoning, a mother is loving, but also demanding; tough as well as flexible; able to embody both divine mercy and divine judgment.... She was able to look into the mirror and see herself and her daughters as powerful even as they committed themselves to lives of service. She managed for most of her life to be what many of us hope eventually to become, self-accepting, aware of life's bleak realities without being defined by them, and so quietly self-confident that it seems not to have occurred to her that she would not be able to do what needed to be done....

The word that dominates her writings is *kindness*, the notion that people can teach more effectively, pray more openly, and act in the world more compellingly insofar as they remember to be tender, encouraging, loving. The ability of hers to *enable* her followers by encouraging them to trust themselves is no small thing to emulate in these times of confusion....

Mary Jo Weaver

RESPONSORY

Angela joyfully served others for the glory of God alone. —**Angela.**
She lived in wisdom and holiness; —**for the**...
Glory to you, Source of all Being, Eternal Word and Holy Spirit.
　—**Angela**...

CANTICLE

Ant　Cling together with the bonds of love, esteeming, helping
　　and supporting one another in Christ Jesus.*

INTERCESSIONS:

O God, through your daughter Angela, you promised to provide
for all our needs. In confidence we turn to you and say:
　　　　　　Hear our prayer and help us.

Angela told us that the more united we are, the more God is
among us;
　　—teach us to overcome the obstacles of prejudice,
　　　selfishness, and fear, and to enable all people to know
　　　that you are present to them.
Angela worked to live and teach your gospel;
　　—help all missionaries and teachers to spread your reign
　　　by word and action.
You blessed Angela with the gift of understanding the
scriptures;
　　—grant us the grace to know and live your word.
Many and varied are the ways you are served by those who
claim Angela as their foundress;
　　—give the Church unity in its diversity and trust in the
　　　presence of your Spirit.

PRAYER: Loving God, in St. Angela you give us an example of
　　　　　　prayerful and dedicated service to your people. May
　　　　　　her prayers for us help us to live your gospel as
　　　　　　witnesses to your presence in the world. We ask this
　　　　　　through her intercession and the intercession of all
　　　　　　her faithful followers who now live with you. Amen.

* Excerpts based on her writings.

January 28
MAISIE WARD

Maisie Ward, born into a distinguished family January 4, 1889, was a publisher, writer, activist, and street-corner preacher. With her husband, Frank Sheed, she founded the Catholic publishing house, Sheed & Ward, to bring Catholic thought out of the cloister and the lecture room into everyday life. She wrote many books on modernism, the lives of the saints, Robert Browning, and others, and was an avid promoter of the proposition that "God matters." For fifty years, as a member of the Catholic Evidence Guild, she was a regular speaker in Hyde Park or in Times Square, defending or explaining Roman Catholicism. She was a tireless activist, whether promoting the works of social reformers like Dorothy Day, or working for her own organization, the Catholic Housing Aid Society in England. The most prominent woman in the Roman Catholic publishing world, Maisie Ward died January 28, 1975.

MORNING/EVENING PRAYER

(Psalms for Feasts, p. 75, or p. 77)

Ant 1 Christ is the light of every person.*

Ant 2 We need not lose the natural to gain the supernatural.*

Ant 3 In heaven I hope to meet many who were inside the City of God unrecognized.*

REFLECTION/SHARING

I sometimes cherish a fancy that the psalmist's promise is fulfilled and that in an old age of unusual health and strength there has been given back to me something of "the years that the locusts have eaten."*

RESPONSORY

My heart overflows with a goodly theme —**My heart**...
My tongue is like the pen of a ready scribe; —**with a**...
Glory to you, Source of all Being, Eternal Word and Holy Spirit.
    —**My heart**...

CANTICLE

Ant This is the Christian humanism to which I most fully
    subscribe—not to decry the riches of this world because

we believe in another, not to reject the temporal for fear of
losing life eternal.*

INTERCESSIONS:

O God, you granted Maisie Ward a life long openness to truth;
   —help us to lay aside our preconceptions when faced with
   the mystery and challenge of your unconditional love.
Maisie was a loving wife and mother, and her dedication went
beyond her family through lectures given around the world;
   —awaken in us the call to discipleship and the courage to
   follow it.
Author, publisher, poet, and street preacher, Maisie felt herself
united in mission with those dedicated to a life of prayer;
   —help all in your vineyard to realize their unity in Christ.
Maisie endeavored to facilitate a union of Christian churches
and dreamed of a bonding of East and West;
   —grant people of every faith throughout the world a
   deepening respect for one another.
Maisie looked forward to "this world transformed into a new
heaven and a new earth—but still this world in its innermost
values";
   —encourage all who long and labor to preserve this planet.

PRAYER: O God, you enriched the life of Maisie Ward with an
            abundance of gifts, and she responded with deep
            generosity. We thank you for all that you have given
            to us through her, and we ask for the grace to let
            our own talents give glory to you and support
            to others. Help us to look beyond our own
            limited boundaries of family or interest. Give
            encouragement and new inspiration to those who
            work for ecumenism—for the unity for which Jesus
            prayed. We ask this in his name. Amen.

* Excepts taken from *Unfinished Business* © 1964 by Maisie Ward, Sheed &
Ward, New York.

February 1
ST. BRIGID OF KILDARE

St. Brigid of Kildare was born about the year 450 in a place called Faughart on the east coast of Ireland. A Christian by birth through her mother, a slave, she was also knowledgeable of the Druid ways of her father. With several other young women, she began Ireland's first convent of nuns and eventually became an abbess governing both women and men. She is a patron saint of Ireland.

MORNING/EVENING PRAYER

(Psalms for Feasts, p. 75, or p. 77)

Ant 1 Since I first fixed my mind on God, I have never taken it off.*

Ant 2 As the outcome of your faith you obtain the salvation of your souls.*

Ant 3 Come to that living stone, rejected by humankind, but in God's sight chosen and precious.*

REFLECTION/SHARING

Brigid's gifts to the Christian world include helping lay the foundations of education for the laity through monastery schools, which developed into the universities of the Middle Ages. Moreover, she gave the women of her country the opportunity to use their energies and intellect in a way previously not open to them. For many generations after her, Kildare would continue to be ruled by a double line of abbesses and abbot-bishops. Only in medieval times were convents placed entirely under the jurisdiction of men.*

RESPONSORY

Wisdom reaches mightily from one end of the earth to the other.
    —**Wisdom**...
She orders all things well, —**from one**...
Glory to you, Source of all Being, Eternal Word and Holy Spirit.
    —**Wisdom**...

CANTICLE

Ant You are a chosen race, a royal priesthood, a holy nation, God's own people.

INTERCESSIONS:

O God, you favored Ireland with the brilliant leadership of St. Brigid;
>—grant all nations a leader after your own heart.

Brigid's love for learning and respect for freedom gave new quality of life to women and to all people;
>—give us the grace to remain open to growth all the days of our lives.

Her holiness was magnified by her deep joy;
>—may our love and dedication to you be so manifest.

Brigid's sweet disposition and delicate ways made her loved by all;
>—help us to meet difficult personalities with patience and understanding.

She was lavish in her love for the poor;
>—let love be the measure of our giving in the fullness of your being.

PRAYER: O God, we praise and thank you for the life of St. Brigid. She gave to the Christian world the foundations of education for the laity and the opportunity for women of Ireland to use their energies and intellect in a way previously not open to them. An "ascetic with a smile," she helped lay the foundations of a golden age of learning and missionary endeavor. May she continue to be a beacon of light and courage to all women who labor to lead others to the freedom of the gospel. We ask this in Jesus' name. Amen.

* Excepts from *Women in Church History* © 1990 by Joanne Turpin; St. Anthony Messenger Press, Cincinnati.

February 10
ST. SCHOLASTICA

St. Scholastica was born at Nursia in Italy in about 480. She and her brother, St. Benedict, originated the two branches of the Benedictine Order, which is still flourishing after fourteen centuries. St. Scholastica's whole life was devoted to "seeking God" and is summed up in the twofold maxim of loving justice and hating iniquity. She died in 547.

MORNING/EVENING PRAYER

(Psalms for Feasts, p. 75, or p. 77

Ant 1 She opens her mouth with wisdom, and the teaching of kindness is on her tongue.

Ant 2 Let us love one another, because love is of God.

Ant 3 Make my joy complete by your unanimity, praising the one love, united in Spirit and ideals.

REFLECTION/SHARING

My heart overflows with a goodly theme;...
my tongue is like the pen of a ready scribe.
You love righteousness and hate wickedness.
Therefore God, your God, has anointed you
with the oil of gladness above your companions.
Hear, O daughter, consider, and incline your ear;
forget your people and your parents' house;...
I will cause your name to be celebrated in all generations.

(Psalm 45:1, 7,10, 17)

RESPONSORY

I rejoice heartily in my God in whom is the joy of my soul.
  —I rejoice...
For God has clothed me with the robe of salvation; —in my...
Glory to you, Source of all Being, Eternal Word and Holy Spirit.
  —I rejoice...

CANTICLE

Ant We have come to know and believe in the love God has for us.

INTERCESSIONS:

To those who are pure of heart you manifest yourself, O God. In joyful expectation, we pray:

Prepare our minds and our lips to praise your holy name.

Through the intercession of Scholastica, teach us to pray and to trust in your care for us;
   —teach us to live by the law of love.
Your servant Scholastica pondered your word and knew the value of work;
   —give us the grace always to be people of prayer and to do our work with reverence and creativity.
Scholastica had a deep love for her brother, Benedict;
   —grant that all families may grow closer in love and trust.
Bless all who derive their rule of life from Benedict and Scholastica;
   —keep them faithful to their calling and let them also bear fruit in abundant life for the church.

PRAYER: Loving God, in your daughter, Scholastica, love was stronger than adherence to rule, and you heard her prayer because of her great trust in you. Bless all those who have been gifted with the charism of Scholastica: a gift to the Church of prayer and universal charity. In your mercy, raise up in our day those who are so dedicated to you, that they, too, will guide and nourish all who seek you in spirit and in truth. This we ask in Jesus, who is your Incarnate Word. Amen.

March 3
BLESSED KATHARINE DREXEL, SBS

Katharine Drexel was born in Philadelphia on November 26, 1858. Through her father, a well-known banker and philanthropist, Katharine learned early on that wealth was to be shared with those in need. When she experienced the destitution of Native Americans, she began her lifelong vocation of serving them. In 1891, she founded the Sisters of the Blessed Sacrament whose mission was to share the gospel with Native and African Americans. She died on March 3, 1955.

MORNING/EVENING PRAYER

(Psalms for Feasts, p. 75, or p. 77)

Ant 1 I want to enter into and be permeated with Jesus' desire to save all—all the world throughout the centuries.*

Ant 2 It is easy to see [Jesus] when our net is full of fish, but hard to recognize him when we have caught nothing.*

Ant 3 Out of our common todays and yesterdays, we are building for eternity.*

REFLECTION/SHARING

We must learn from our loving Savior how we may show kindness by listening, by making leisure for those who are in want of comfort, and by not interrupting nor answering others before we have patiently heard all.*

...If I am silent, reverent and humble, God not only speaks for me, but to me in prayer.*

RESPONSORY

Sell what you have and give to the poor. —**Sell what**...
Come follow me; —**and give**...
Glory to you, Source of all Being, Eternal Word and Holy Spirit.
    —**Sell what**...

CANTICLE

Ant The offspring of this intensity of love for our Eucharistic Lord should be a consuming zeal for the gathering of souls into the fold of Christ.*

INTERCESSIONS:

All day long I abide with [Christ] and must watch him whom I am to imitate;*
    —Jesus, help us to keep you in mind and to live in the present moment.

It is only by entering into oneself in prayer and meditation that the soul can be restored to its true poise...and the value of unimportant things be seen in its true light;*
    —Spirit of God, teach us to pray.
It is a lesson we all need—to let alone the things that do not concern us;*
    —O God, teach us the things that are to our peace.
Kind words, by their power of producing happiness, have also a power of producing holiness;*
    —let our words, O God, bear your love and creativity.
Beware of sadness, for it is contrary to love in diminishing and destroying its power of affection;*
    —let us find courage in your cross, Lord Jesus, and joy in
       your resurrection.*

PRAYER: Ever loving God, you called Blessed Katharine Drexel to share the message of the Gospel and the life of the Eucharist with the poor and oppressed among Native and African American peoples. Through her intercession, may we grow in the faith and love that will enable us to be united as sisters and brothers in you. Inspired by her zeal may we strive for greater unity, justice, and peace. We pray this in Jesus' name. Amen.

* Excerpts from her writings.

March 15
ST. LOUISE DE MARILLAC

Louise was born in Paris, France, on August 12, 1591. Her mother died soon after her birth. At an early age Louise was attracted to everything that spoke of poverty, and she loved to help others to ease their burdens in any way she could. When she was seventeen years old she had a desire to become a Poor Clare nun, but her confessor discouraged her due to her frail health and the austere rule of the Capuchin order. In 1613, at the age of twenty-two, she married Antoine Le Gras. After a year of marriage they had a son. Both she and her husband had a love for the poor. When her husband became very ill, she lovingly cared for him and was at his bedside when he died on Christmas Eve, 1625. After the death of her husband, she met Vincent de Paul who became her spiritual director. On November 29, 1633, after years of collaboration, they cofounded the Daughters of Charity. The following year, her desire to commit herself to God by vow was realized.

MORNING/EVENING PRAYER

(Psalms for Feasts, p. 75, or p. 77)

Ant 1 After having seen the beauty of virtue, we must proceed to resolve to practice it; otherwise prayer is not well made.*

Ant 2 The virtue of cordiality should not stand alone for it is in need of another virtue, which is respect.*

Ant 3 Prayer and mortification are two sisters who are so closely united together that one will never be found without the other.

REFLECTION/SHARING

Receiving from Christ the great commandment of charity, we shall once again remember that we can only be evangelizers to the extent that we live and radiate love.*

The art of collaborating with others is a charism one must ask of God in prayer. It was Louise's profound humility that allowed her to acknowledge, accept, and use the gifts and talents of others. Thus the poor were greatly helped because of her gift of collaboration with others for the sake of the church.

RESPONSORY

You have given us an example of love and service; help us to be faithful. **—You have...**
Walk in humility and confidence; **—help us...**
Glory to you, Source of all Being, Eternal Word and Holy Spirit.
    —You have...

CANTICLE

Ant It is into hearts who seek God alone that God is pleased to pour forth the most excellent lights and great graces.*

INTERCESSIONS:

O God, through Louise, you taught us a deeper love and respect for the poor and so we entreat you:
Help us to serve them, respecting their dignity.

Christ Jesus, you inspired the daughters of Louise to be women of compassion and empathy in their service to humankind;
   —help us to grow in mercy and understanding.
Loving Creator, we thank you for the example of untiring collaboration of Louise with Vincent in the formation of works of charity;
   —may we follow her example in our service of the church.
Louise transformed adversity into positive energy for the service of the unfortunate;
   —help us to see with the eyes of faith and the mind of Christ.
O God, send laborers into your harvest to mirror the gospel values of justice and love of Christ;
   —may our lives give you glory and praise.

PRAYER: O God, you inspired Louise de Marillac with the spirit of charity for the poor. In response to her call, she envisioned a new way of living the vows. Her daughters' cloister would be the streets of the city or the wards of hospitals, their cell a hired room, and their grill, obedience. Grant us the grace to serve those whose lives we touch with the same spirit of love, and may the family of Louise continue to grow and multiply throughout the world. Amen.

* Excerpts taken from *A Woman Named Louise* by Sister Bertrande, DC.

March 25
ANNUNCIATION

MORNING/EVENING PRAYER
(Psalms for Feasts of Our Lady, p. 79)

Ant 1 A virgin shall conceive and bear a child, and the child shall be called Emmanuel (alleluia).

Ant 2 The angel Gabriel said to Mary: Hail, full of grace, the Most High is with you (alleluia).

Ant 3 You have favored the lowliness of your handmaid and have lifted up the powerless (alleluia).

REFLECTION/SHARING

In the sixth month the angel Gabriel was sent from God to a city of Galilee named Nazareth, to a virgin betrothed to a man whose name was Joseph, and the virgin's name was Mary. The angel said to her, "The Holy Spirit will come upon you, and the power of the Most High will overshadow you; therefore the child to be born will be called holy, the Son of God." (Lk 1:26–27, 35)

RESPONSORY

You are the honor of our race, you are the joy of our people.
    —You are...
The promise has been fulfilled; **—you are...**
Glory to you, Source of all Being, Eternal Word and Holy Spirit.
    —You are...

CANTICLE

Ant I am God's handmaid. Be it done to me according to your word.

INTERCESSIONS:

O God, Mary heard your word and entered into the mystery of redemption;
    —give us the grace to follow the lure of your call to growth.

Her fiat brings salvation to the world;
  —let all of our choices promote life and give you praise and
    glory.
Mary's motherhood brought her martyrdom of heart;
  —bless all parents who must bear deep suffering with and
    for their children.
Mary went in haste to support and to share the mystery of new
life with her cousin Elizabeth;
  —teach us how to share with others the fruit of your Spirit
    in our lives.
Your mercies, O God, endure from age to age, working marvels
among your people;
  —free all women who are in bondage and who lead lives less
    than human.

PRAYER: O God, in the fullness of time you called the virgin
Mary to be the mother of Jesus. As we celebrate this
mystery of the annunciation, grant us the grace to
open our lives to all that you call us to be. Give us
the mind and heart of Mary, that we too may bear
Christ to the world. We ask this through Jesus
Christ, the Incarnate Word and our Redeemer.
Amen.

March 26
CAROLINE CHISHOLM*

Caroline (Jones) Chisholm, the Emigrants' Friend, born on a farm near
Northampton, England, in 1808, forced the British government to change its
policies regarding settlement in Australia. Caroline married Archibald
Chisholm, a Scottish soldier in the East India Company's army, and was the
mother of seven children. Archibald promised to support Caroline in her
determination to help people in need. She set up hostels and arranged
employment for young girls and families, even traveling miles overland with
them to ensure the integrity of the employers. Caroline helped to found a
scheme by which emigrants could borrow money for fares to Australia and
purchase land and equipment on arrival. Her achievements were the product
of single-minded vision and compassion, augmented by a strong Christian
faith. She helped thousands despite sectarian bitterness and little financial
support. Caroline Chisholm died March 25, 1877.

MORNING/EVENING PRAYER

(Psalms for Feasts, p. 75, or Social Justice, p. 82)

Ant 1 She holds out her hands to the poor; she opens her arms to the needy.

Ant 2 Who shall find a valiant woman? Far and to the uttermost coasts is the price of her.

Ant 3 Cast your bread upon the water; at long last you will find it again.

REFLECTION/SHARING

"During Lent and Easter of that year I suffered much, but on the Easter Sunday I was enabled, at the altar of Our Lord, to make an offering of my talents to the God who gave them. I promised to know neither country nor creed, but to try to serve all justly and impartially. I asked only to be enabled to keep these poor girls from being tempted, by their need, to mortal sin; and resolved that to accomplish this, I would in every way sacrifice my feelings...surrender all comfort...nor in fact consider my own wishes or feelings but wholly devote myself to the work I had in hand.

"I felt my offering was accepted and God's blessing was on my work; but it was [God's] will to permit many serious difficulties to be thrown in my way, and to conduct me through a rugged path of deep humiliation."**

RESPONSORY

Wisdom is bright and does not grow dim. —**Wisdom**...
By those who love her she is readily seen, —**and does not**...
Glory to you, Source of all Being, Eternal Word and Holy Spirit.
   —**Wisdom**...

CANTICLE

Ant Put your hope in God, be strong. Let your heart be bold! Put your hope in the One who saves.

INTERCESSIONS:

O God, mindful of those in need, we pray to you as we
commemorate this courageous woman:
   Let your mercy be upon us as we place our trust in you.

Christ Jesus, you restored the dignity of women and numbered
them among your friends;
   —may we be watchful and ready to meet the needs of women
   in our society.
Christ Jesus, you said "Come to me all who labor and are
heavily burdened";
   —console and comfort those who suffer from exploitation
   and oppression.
Christ Jesus, you raise up women and men to meet the needs
of every age;
   —raise up in our day women like Caroline Chisholm, fearless
   in their following of you.

PRAYER: O God, we thank you for the life of Caroline
         Chisholm, who rescued countless immigrant women
         from degradation, restored their dignity, and brought
         them new hope. May her courage and determination
         inspire us in our efforts to overcome the evils we see
         around us. We ask this in the name of Jesus who
         suffered and died that all may have a better quality
         of life. Amen.

* Composed by the Sisters of St. Joseph, Australia.
** Excerpt taken from *The Emigrants' Friend* by Joanna Bogle, Fowler Wright
Books, Gracewing House, Herefordshire.

March 30
THEA BOWMAN, FSPA

Thea Bowman was a member of the Franciscan Sisters of Perpetual
Adoration. On March 30, 1990, she died of cancer at the age of fifty-two. Sr.
Thea was a distinguished lecturer and is best known for her work as an
evangelist in promoting intercultural awareness. She received numerous

awards, but her greatness is found in her joy during affliction, her courage, her simplicity, and her acceptance of herself and others.

MORNING/EVENING PRAYER

(Psalms for Feasts, p. 75, or p. 77)

Ant 1 O God, you put a song in her heart and on her lips.

Ant 2 God of Wisdom, teach us who we are and whose we are.

Ant 3 We are one body, one spirit—all of us in Christ Jesus.

REFLECTION/SHARING

"Go tell it on the mountain,
Over the hills and everywhere,...
When I was a sinner I prayed
I asked the Lord to help me and He showed me the way.
When I was a seeker,
I sought both night and day
I asked the Lord to help me and He taught me to pray...".

RESPONSORY

I feel like an eagle in the air, a long way from home. —**I feel**...
Restless until I rest in you; —**a long**...
Glory to you, Source of all Being, Eternal Word and Holy Spirit.
   —**I feel**...

CANTICLE

Ant There is neither slave nor free, male nor female; for you
   are all one in Christ Jesus.

INTERCESSIONS:

Thea called herself an "old folks' child" because she learned
from the wisdom of her elders;
   —teach us to treasure the elderly and to learn how to listen
   to them.
She saw herself as a "bridge over troubled waters";
   —may we learn to bridge the differences between races,
   cultures, religions, and nationalities.

She encouraged her students to be the best they could be;
    —enable us to liberate others to be themselves.
Thea shared the story of her people in song and dance;
    —give us the grace to use our gifts to reach out to others.
Her faith, courage, and inner peace enabled her to face her
impending death;
    —may all those diagnosed with terminal illness know the
    love that can sustain them in their final journey.

PRAYER: O God, your son, Jesus, lived among us that we
might know how to be like you. We thank you for
those like Thea Bowman, who throughout the
centuries have witnessed to your love for the lonely,
the alienated, and the afflicted—for those who teach
us that all you ask is for us to be our best selves—
persons made in your image and likeness—your
beloved children in whom you are well pleased. We
ask this is Jesus' name. Amen.

April 7
ST. JULIE BILLIART

Julie Billiart, born in France in 1751, founded the congregation of Sisters of
Notre Dame de Namur. Though afflicted by many physical sufferings and the
political unrest of the French Revolution, Julie Billiart was a woman of
courage with outstanding faith. She died April 7, 1816.

MORNING/EVENING PRAYER

(Psalms for Feasts, p. 75, or p. 77)

Ant 1 If you would follow me, take up your cross.

Ant 2 All will go right or not; if it does not go right, the good
God will open a way for us.*

Ant 3 May our good Jesus and his holy cross live in us!*

REFLECTION/SHARING

Time is a great teacher. I like to let it pass: it will teach us many things. I go on quietly from day to day. I want to wait on God, to look at [God], to follow [God]. My heart utters only one cry, "My God, what wouldst Thou have me do?" "Mary, my good Mother, save me!" I hope God will bless the inspirations with which [God] has inspired me.*

RESPONSORY

Do not be frightened, God will never fail you. —**Do not...**
In joy or adversity, —**God...**
Glory to you, Source of all Being, Eternal Word and Holy Spirit.
    —**Do not...**

CANTICLE

Ant As gold in the furnace, God proved her.

INTERCESSIONS:

You use the weak ones of the earth to accomplish your works,
O God, and so we pray:
    Blessed are they who suffer persecution for your sake.

O God, through the intercession of Julie Billiart;
    —may all threatened by revolutions and political unrest
        know the peace the world cannot give.
For nearly twenty years of her adult life, Julie was a cripple;
    —give courage to those who are injured and physically
        disabled.
She was a "soul of prayer" and a woman of sound common
sense;
    —help us all to use our gifts of nature and grace for your
        glory.
Julie persevered in her dedication to your call in spite of civil,
ecclesiastic, and domestic persecution;
    —comfort all who suffer misunderstanding as they follow
        the guidance of the Spirit.

PRAYER: Most loving God, you blessed your daughter, Julie, with humility and wisdom in the midst of struggle and misunderstanding. Through her, many came to know your love and concern. Bless her followers, the Sisters of Notre Dame de Namur, that they may continue the wodrk you began in her. We ask this in the names of Jesus and his mother, Mary. Amen.

* Excerpts from her writings.

April 17
ANNA DENGEL, SCMM

Anna Marie Dengel was born on March 16, 1892, in Steeg, Austria. In her late teens, she heard that women and children were dying needlessly in another land because their customs would not allow them to be treated by men. She responded by becoming a doctor and eventually founding the Medical Mission Sisters, a community for whom she obtained permission to "practice medicine in its full scope." When Mother Dengel died in April, 1980, the Medical Mission Sisters were serving the sick and needy on five continents, and through them the vision of their foundress continues to expand throughout the world today.

MORNING/EVENING PRAYER

(Psalms for Feasts, p. 75, or p. 77)

Ant 1 The impossible of today is the work of tomorrow.*

Ant 2 I was fire and flame.... I was determined to become a mission doctor.*

Ant 3 A religious community has a task to do...to be an arm of the Church, to reach out in the name of Christ to the hundred and one human needs.*

REFLECTION/SHARING

A woman was going down from Jerusalem to Jericho, and she fell among robbers, who stripped her and beat her, and departed, leaving her half dead. A foreigner, as she journeyed, came to where she was, and when she saw her, she had compassion, and went to her and bound up her wounds.

RESPONSORY

Every person has an inherent right to live a fully human life.
　　—**Every person**...
Justice is essential to the healing that enables all people;
　　—**to live**...
Glory to you, Source of all Being, Eternal Word and Holy Spirit.
　　—**Every person**...

CANTICLE

Ant All the ends of the earth have seen the saving power of
　　God.

INTERCESSIONS:

Throughout her life, Anna Dengel had a passion for
possibilities;
　　—O God, increase our faith.
Mother Dengel taught her sisters to be a healing presence
among people in need;
　　—help us to remove anything in our lives that blocks your
　　　life-giving Spirit.
She dreamed of a world where no boundaries existed, where
women and men, Christian and Muslim...all people had access
to what would make them fully human;
　　—Spirit of God, open our hearts and minds to the reality of
　　　your Presence in every person.
Her deep compassion inspired others to serve the sick in
cultures where women had formerly been left untreated;
　　—Jesus our Savior, awaken us to the hidden needs of others.
To the advantage of those she taught and served, Mother
Dengel combined religious life in the Church with medical
professionalism;
　　—Creator God, give us the generosity and perseverance to do
　　　all things well.

PRAYER: O God, Anna Dengel transformed the challenges of her life and the needs of others into a means of healing and salvation for people throughout the world. Her compassion and deep faith enabled her to break through ecclesiastic and cultural barriers to allow religious women to serve the needy as medical doctors. Through her intercession, we ask for the wisdom and courage we need to grant all women and men their true dignity in the human family. We ask this for the praise and glory of your name. Amen.

* From her writings.

April 29
ST. CATHERINE OF SIENA

Catherine was born in 1347 and as a young girl entered the Third Order of St. Dominic. She worked for peace between cities, fought for the rights of the Pope in Rome, and was a dominant figure of the fourteenth century. Though semiliterate, her experience of mystical theology was such that she has been named a Doctor of the Church.

MORNING/EVENING PRAYER

(Psalms for Feasts, p. 75, or p. 77)

Ant 1 No virtue can have life in it except from love, and love is nursed and mothered by humility.*

Ant 2 It was love that made you create us and give us being.*

Ant 3 We are your image, and now by making yourself one with us you have become our image.*

REFLECTION/SHARING

You, eternal Trinity, are the craftsman; and I your handiwork have come to know that you are in love with the beauty of what you have made, since you made of me a new creation in the blood of your Son.*

O abyss! O eternal Godhead! O deep sea! What more could you have given me than the gift of your very self?*

RESPONSORY

You, O Lord Jesus, call me and I'm coming to you.* —**You...**
Through your mercy, —**I'm coming...**
Glory to you, Source of all Being, Eternal Word and Holy Spirit.
 —**You...**

CANTICLE

Ant To love is to insert one's self in the nature of God, who is
 the way, the truth, and the life, who is goodness and
 peace.*

INTERCESSIONS:

O God, your daughter Catherine was a woman of great courage
who challenged the Church she loved;
 —may the whole Church always be open to your grace and
 truth.
In her life, she was known as a woman of peace;
 —may all who are estranged be reconciled in Christ who is
 our peace.
Catherine was devoured by hunger for your honor O God, and
the salvation of your people;
 —enkindle our desires for you and for the good of others.
Through Catherine, you called the laity and the clergy to work
together as the people of God;
 —further the work of dialogue and ministry that each
 person's gifts may be used for the sake of the gospel.
Though a victim of slander and malicious talk, Catherine
forgave those who spoke ill of her;
 —give us the grace to forgive others as we have been so
 graciously forgiven.

PRAYER: Loving God, you strengthened your servant,
 Catherine, a woman of courage and deep faith, to
 challenge the leaders of the Church of her day for
 the sake of unity and peace. Bless all those who
 challenge us in our complacency; give us the spirit of
 Jesus to truly love and reverence one another that
 we may be one family united in Christ. Amen.

* Excerpts from her writings.

May 8
JULIAN OF NORWICH

Julian of Norwich, an anonymous woman, was a fourteenth-century mystic. She lived as a recluse in a cell attached to the church of St. Julian of Norwich. Her writings have been a source of inspiration throughout the centuries, and they reveal a contemplative woman who is a reliable spiritual guide for those who follow the spiritual path.

MORNING/EVENING PRAYER

(Psalms for Feasts, p. 75, or p. 77)

Ant 1 You will see yourself, that every kind of thing will be well.*

Ant 2 We shall rejoice only in our blessed Savior, Jesus, and trust in him for everything.*

Ant 3 By contrition we are made clean, by compassion we are made ready, and by true longing for God we are made worthy.*

REFLECTION/SHARING

I contemplated the work of all the blessed Trinity, in which contemplation I saw and understood these three properties: the property of the fatherhood, and the property of the motherhood, and the property of the Lordship in one God....*

For the almighty truth of the Trinity is our Father, for he made us and keeps us in him. And the deep wisdom of the Trinity is our Mother, in whom we are enclosed. And the high goodness of the Trinity is our Lord, and in him we are enclosed and he is in us.*

RESPONSORY

Mercy is a sweet, gracious operation in love, mingled with plentiful compassion.* —**Mercy**...
For mercy works, protecting us, turning everything to good for us;* —**mingled**...
Glory to you, Source of all Being, Eternal Word and Holy Spirit. —**Mercy**...

CANTICLE

Ant For I saw most truly that where Jesus Christ appears,
peace is received and wrath has no place.*

INTERCESSIONS:

O God of tender compassion, we trust in you at every moment.
We turn to you and pray:
        O God, have mercy upon us.

You, O God, are our true peace and safe protector;
—may all who experience the horrors of war and violence
find comfort in your outstretched arm.
Jesus, you have compassion on us because of our sin;
—may all who are estranged know the peace of your
reconciling love.
You take heed not only of great and noble things, but also in
those which are little and small;
—may all know the joy of your providential love and care.
You invite us, O God, to be united with you in prayer;
—in you alone, we live, and move, and have our being.
Jesus lived in the desert for forty days, praying and fasting;
—bless all women who are called to be hermits and
anchoresses.

PRAYER: O Compassionate One, you rejoice that you are our
Father, and you rejoice that you are our Mother.
Give us the faith and courage to truly believe in the
absolute truth of your tender mercy for us and for all
humanity. We ask this in the name of Jesus, our
Savior and brother. Amen.

* Excerpts from her writings.

May 14
VEN. MOTHER THEODORE GUERIN, SP

Mother Theodore (Anne-Therese) Guerin was born in Etables, France, October 2, 1798. In 1823, after years of opposition and painful waiting, family circumstances left her free to join the Sisters of Providence at Ruille-sur-Loir. In her native France, Sr. Theodore distinguished herself by her inspired teaching and loving care of the sick-poor. In 1840, she was chosen to establish the Sisters of Providence at St. Mary-of-the-Woods, Indiana. This mission, carried out amid the hardships of pioneer life, entailed labors and crosses that she bore with invincible charity and fortitude. Her life gives testimony not only to gifted administrative ability but also to heroic faith, profound humility, and untiring zeal for souls.

MORNING/EVENING PRAYER

(Psalms for Feasts, p. 75, or p. 77)

Ant 1 Be assured that in leaving the past to the mercy of God and the future to [God's] providence, you will derive from your offering very great peace and consolation.*

Ant 2 The spirit of faith consists in doing our actions for God and in [God's] presence.*

Ant 3 Oh how good a thing is silence. It is a sovereign remedy for nearly every kind of evil and the means to acquire a great many virtues.*

REFLECTION/SHARING

What shall we offer today in union with Jesus?... Ah! There remains something else...which, perhaps, we have not yet given to God, some other goods which I will call future events. For example, we will give to God our choice of the kind of death we shall have; our desires for certain employments; our reputation; our health—to be sick or well, useful or useless, it will be equally indifferent to us, as it will be also to have consolation or aridity in our prayers, repose or temptations; all we shall leave sweetly to the providence of God. This will be our offering.*

RESPONSORY

When I am afraid, I put my trust in you, in you whose word I
   praise. —**When I...**
In you I trust without fear; —**in you whose**...
Glory to you, Source of all Being, Eternal Word and Holy Spirit.
   —**When I...**

CANTICLE

Ant Perfect abandonment of ourselves in all things for the
   future requires great courage,...but we ought to aspire
   to it.*

INTERCESSIONS:

O God, you gave the gift of holiness to your servant, Mother
Theodore;
   —grant us the light, grace, and strength we need to lead
      lives holy and blameless in your sight.
With great courage, Mother Theodore endured her crosses in
union with your son in his sufferings;
   —strengthen us as we try to learn the lessons of your love
      and the cross.
O God, through your servant you brought your gospel to your
children in a foreign land;
   —help us to respond courageously in true service to your
      people that with them we may journey toward a world of
      justice, love, and peace.
Mother Theodore taught that love and not fear is the guiding
force of education;
   —bless all those dedicated to the profession of teaching; may
      they further God's providence through works of love as
      they instruct others in their academic pursuits.
Provident God, Mother Theodore found you in the forests of
Indiana, offering you all that she possessed; trusting in your
providential guidance; hoping that through her life and the
lives of her sisters, faith and knowledge would grow.
   —Once again we reach out to you, offering our lives for the
      continued effort of building providence in our world today.

PRAYER: O God, whose name is Providence, and whose face
is always turned toward our world, we thank you
for your constant fidelity. Our path into the future
at times seems unclear, yet we turn to you with
patience and trust. Leaning upon your goodness and
strength, we believe we will always be sustained and
supported. Hear and answer us in Jesus' name.
Amen.

* Excerpts from her writings.

May 21
IRENE McCORMACK, RSJ*

Irene McCormack was born in Trayning, a rural area of Western Australia in
1938. Small in stature, she had an almost permanent smile and a great
sense of fun. She loved golf and dancing and was an avid sports fan and
critic. After thirty years as a teacher in Catholic schools in Australia, Irene, a
Sister of St. Joseph, volunteered to work with the poor of Peru. On the night
of May 21, 1991, Irene and four men from the village—Noe Palacios Blancas,
Agustin Vento Morales, Pedro Pando Llanos, and Alfredo Morales Torres—
were murdered by terrorists.

MORNING/EVENING PRAYER

(Psalms for Social Justice, p. 82; Feasts, p. 75)

Ant 1 As the clay is in the potter's hand, so you are in mine.

Ant 2 You feed us with the finest wheat.

Ant 3 Come, my beloved, let us go forth into the fields, and
lodge in the villages.

REFLECTION/SHARING

To continue to spiritualize what it means to be poor, and not to
work with the poor in a Third World situation, is for me a
rationalization, a way of evading the real world. My fidelity to
the Lord can no longer allow me to do this.

However, my involvement with Peruvians whose needs are at
the most elementary level of physical survival is just another

facet of our Josephite charism. Why I have been called to live out this facet of our charism rather than another is in the realm of mystery, just as was my original call to Religious Life. But, as in the original call, I have no doubt that it is God's gift.

I do not want anyone's pity, or admiration, just due recognition and thanks for the Lord of Life at work in the life of all of us.**

RESPONSORY

Bless the work of our hands, O God; bless the work of our hands.
    —**Bless the**...
Give us hearts of compassion that we may serve you; —**bless the**...
Glory to you, Source of all Being, Eternal Word and Holy Spirit.
    —**Bless the**...

CANTICLE

Ant I have given you as a covenant to the people. God will save
        the poor from oppression and violence.

INTERCESSIONS:

How beautiful upon the mountains are the feet of the messenger who announces peace, who brings good news; and so we pray:

Jesus, make us free!

In an ordinary and down-to-earth way Irene's warmth and faith brought your love to the poor in Peru;
        —may we, rather than simply spiritualize what it means to
        be poor, have a *concrete* and *authentic* love for your poor.
In her farming background Irene learned a dependence on the earth and your providence;
        —give us an awareness of the fragile balance between relying
        on our own resources and trusting in yours.
Irene lifted the spirits of the children of Peru through teaching them to play and through her love of music and dance;
        —help us to share our talents in a more practical and human
        way.

Among an oppressed people, Irene chose life;
  —may Jesus, the free man, be the inspiration and core of our
    works for peace and justice in our world.
Like Jesus, Irene was buried in a borrowed grave among the
people she loved;
  —help us to see that not only in life, but in death, we
    minister to each other.

PRAYER: O God, the life of Irene challenges us to be authentic
         in showing your love. Finding the pearl of great price
         among the poor of Peru, she gave all. Help us to
         accept all as gift, to choose life without fear, and to
         live wholeheartedly each day. We ask this in Jesus'
         name. Amen.

* Composed by the Sisters of St. Joseph, Australia.
** Excerpt from Irene's address to the Congregation at her missioning Mass,
January, 1987.

May 25
ST. MADELEINE SOPHIE BARAT

Madeleine Sophie Barat, born at Burgundy, December 12, 1779, founded the
Society of the Sacred Heart. From her earliest years, she felt called to be
a nun. In spite of her personal illness and many difficulties, the Society
flourished. Madeleine Sophie was known for her common sense, courage,
and kindness. Her apostolic zeal and her contemplative spirituality were the
cornerstones of the Society she founded. Madeleine Sophie died May 25,
1865.

MORNING/EVENING PRAYER

(Psalms for Feasts, p. 75, or p. 77)

Ant 1 It is the interior spirit that gives life and fruitfulness to
everything.*

Ant 2 The proof of true love is forgetfulness of self and one's
own interests.*

Ant 3 What difference does it make how you pray, provided
your heart is seeking the One whom you love?*

REFLECTION/SHARING

...Be pious, but with a piety which puts duty before exercises of pure devotion. Be firm against the world and human respect. Be simple and modest.... Don't judge, be kindly in thought. Don't just be good; be lovable, with that lovability which is both energetic and thoughtful of others which you will find in the strong and sweet Heart of Jesus.*

RESPONSORY

O God, let us drink with joy from your life-giving waters. —**O God...**
Cleanse our hearts and our minds; —**with joy**...
Glory to you, Source of all Being, Eternal Word and Holy Spirit.
   —**O God...**

CANTICLE

Ant Let us have no memory but to remember, no heart but to
   bless, no strength but to serve.*

INTERCESSIONS:

O God, we pray to you as we commemorate this holy woman:
   May you be glorified in your saints.

Christ Jesus, you invited the little children to come to you;
   —may all children know your love and concern by the
      respect given to them.
Through the intercession of Madeleine Sophie;
   —bless all those responsible for the education of children.
O God, in Madeleine Sophie, you gave us a model of leadership;
   —may all administrators be given the gift of wisdom and
      moderation.
O God, you gave Madeleine Sophie a great love of humility;
   —let all recognize you as the source and giver of all that we
      are and possess.

PRAYER: O God, we bless you for the life of Madeleine Sophie.
         We thank you for all that you accomplished through
         her. Bless all those who follow and are guided by her
         inspiration as they continue your work in this world.

May they be faithful to her spirit and counsels. This we ask in the name of Jesus. Amen.

* Excerpts from her writings.

June 1
HELEN KELLER

Helen Keller was born in Tuscumbia, Alabama, in 1880. When nineteen months old, she was stricken with a disease that left her blind and deaf. Through the help and heroic determination of her teacher, Anne Sullivan, Helen was able to overcome her disabilities. She became an eloquent speaker, spoke several languages, and lectured all over the world. Her life has been an inspiration to all. Helen Keller died June 1, 1968.

MORNING/EVENING PRAYER

(Psalms for Feasts, p. 75, or p. 77)

Ant 1 Out of the depths I cry to you, O God; hear the sound of my pleading.

Ant 2 The water that I shall give them will become in them a spring of living water, welling up to eternal life.

Ant 3 Blessed are those who have not seen and have believed.

REFLECTION/SHARING

W-A-T-E-R: That living word awakened my soul, gave it light, hope, joy, set it free! There were barriers still, it is true, but barriers that could in time be swept away.*

Faith, like philosophy, endows me with a unity I miss in the chaos of material experience devoid of sight and hearing. But like everyone else I have eyes in my soul. Through faith I create the world I gaze upon; I make my own day and night, tint the clouds with iridescent fires, and behold! a midnight is strewn with stars.*

RESPONSORY

Seek and you shall find; knock and it shall be opened. **—Seek**...
Ask and you shall receive; **—knock**...
Glory to you, Source of all Being, Eternal Word and Holy Spirit.
  —Seek...

CANTICLE

Ant Eye has not seen, nor ear heard, nor has it entered into
    the heart of anyone what you have prepared for those who
    love you.

INTERCESSIONS:

God has done wonderful things through women and men of all
ages. Let us give praise for the marvelous life of Helen Keller:
  Wonderful are your works, O God.

O God, you have created us in your image; you have created us
free;
    —through the manifestation of vibrant life in Helen Keller,
      give us a reverence for our own and all life, and keep us
      grateful to you.
Our lives are replete with the mysteries of joy and suffering;
    —help us to see your loving care and call in both, and to
      remain faithful to you to the end.
In the face of a "living death," Helen Keller was able to choose
life;
    —give us the grace to cherish every aspect of our lives and to
      let hope in you be our guide through adversity.
Helen Keller found new life through the patient care of others;
    —remembering your mercy to us, let us bear with one
      another in our journey to wholeness.
Your servant, Helen Keller, transformed her cross into a gift for
the world;
    —bless us, too, with the insight and creativity to bring life to
      ourselves and others out of the things that afflict us.

PRAYER: O God, we thank you for making known to the world
        the valiant life of Helen Keller. Let her love for life
        give courage to those who live in the shadow of

death. Let her courage in the face of deprivation spur us on to engage the challenges of our lives with hope and creativity. Teach us how to help one another, and give us the faith to embrace and revere the mystery of creation. Through it all may you be praised forever, Source of Life, Savior and Sanctifier of the world. Amen.

* Excerpts from her writings.

June 5
MARGARET ANNA CUSACK
(Foundress of the Sisters of St. Joseph of Peace)

Margaret Anna Cusack was born May 6, 1829, in Dublin, Ireland. A strict Anglican, Margaret Anna eventually entered an Anglican convent of Sisters. Influenced by the Oxford movement, Margaret Anna converted to Catholicism in 1858 and shortly thereafter entered a Poor Clare community in Ireland. She dedicated herself to writing, especially on behalf of the liberation of women and children who were victims of oppression in the Church and society. To broaden the scope of her work, she founded the Sisters of St. Joseph of Peace and came to the United States to help young Irish women arriving there. Conflict with the Archbishop of New York led other bishops to reject the new community. To preserve it, Margaret Anna severed canonical connections with the Sisters of St. Joseph of Peace in 1888 and returned to England. Abandoned by the Roman Catholic Church, she died with the blessing of the Anglican Church and was buried in Leamington cemetery. Her coffin had a simple inscription, "Margaret Anna Cusack fell asleep, June 5th 1899, aged 70 years."

MORNING/EVENING PRAYER
(Psalms for Social Justice, p. 84; Feasts, p. 75)

Ant 1 They took up the cry that I was interfering in politics! God help me, all the politics I cared for was to feed the hungry.*

Ant 2 If I had been assassinated, to have died for the cause of charity would have been a happy end to my troubled life.*

Ant 3 I at last decided to withdraw from a work which it was quite evident I should not be allowed to accomplish under any circumstances.*

REFLECTION/SHARING

Give women their rights then, for these rights are justice— justice to men as well as to women, for the interests of men and women cannot be separated. Let women have the possession and the control of their property; it is a necessary right for the rich as well as for the poor. (*Women's Work*, 1874)*

The time is quite passed when women could be told that they had no business with politics or that they were incapable of giving an opinion on public affairs. (*Women's Work*, 1874)*

RESPONSORY

I have put my Spirit upon her, she will bring forth justice to the nations. —**I have put**...
A bruised reed she will not break nor quench the smoking flax; —**she will**...
Glory to you, Source of all Being, Eternal Word and Holy Spirit. —**I have put**...

CANTICLE

Ant Those who think it is a light matter to leave all things for conscience sake know little indeed what it cost me at my age, and in my peculiar circumstances to obey the call of God.*

INTERCESSIONS:

Because she chose to be practical in carrying out her Christianity, Margaret Anna Cusack went down in the eyes of her contemporaries as a failure, only to be recognized today as a prophet of Church and society;**
    —O God, help us to recognize and affirm the prophets that challenge our institutions in this our day.

Because she criticized publicly the wealth of the Church's hierarchy in contrast to the destitution of the poor, ecclesiastics wanted her silenced;**

> —give us ears to hear what may discomfort our ease for the sake of justice. Comfort those who have endured misunderstanding and wrongful censure.

Margaret Anna foresaw that unless women were educated to be economically and intellectually independent, they would continue to be victimized by society;**

> —grant equal opportunities to women of every nation— particularly women in developing countries that deny them basic human rights.

It was indeed a time of darkness and sorrow to me, and I had not then realized the utter hopelessness of trying to carry on a work to which the bishops were determinedly opposed, no matter what papal sanction I might have;*

> —at times of alienation and rejection, help us to unite our suffering with all the suffering in the world until we know the dawn of resurrection

In leaving the congregation she founded, she wrote: "I have kept them ignorant of what I have done, as far as possible, not because I do not love them, but because I do love them and desire their work to prosper. I know they will not misunderstand me...";**

> —we pray for all members and those associated with the Sisters of St. Joseph of Peace, whose commitment to peace most often flows as a turbulent stream into the waters of prophetic witness.

PRAYER: O God, we thank you for the life of Margaret Anna Cusack who suffered so much for the cause of justice because she risked to speak the truth to those who did not want to hear it. Like Jesus, she endured rejection and alienation from those in authority, and like Jesus, the work that she began has continued to flourish and bring life. Bless all who work to change unjust structures, that they may have the courage and the humility to continue their efforts in spite of opposition so that all peoples

of the earth may have a better quality of life. We ask
this in Jesus' name. Amen.

* Excerpts from her writings.

** This Office was developed primarily from the book *Peace Pays a Price* ©
1990 by Dorothy A. Vidulich, CSJP, Sisters of St. Joseph of Peace,
Washington, D.C.

June 15
EVELYN UNDERHILL
(For John Casteel)

Evelyn Underhill was born in England, December 6, 1875. She was educated
at King's College for Women and married Hubert Stuart Moore in 1907. In
1911, she published *Mysticism* and by 1925 she claimed a vocation to
explain the spiritual life to people living ordinary lives in the world. She was
the first woman to lecture at Oxford. Her book, *Life of the Spirit and the Life
of Today,* was based on these lectures. She was also the first woman in the
Church of England to give a series of talks to priests. She gave retreats to
clergy and other religious professionals. The experience of the First World
War led her to become a confirmed pacifist. She died June 15, 1941. In
1988, the General Convention of the Episcopal Church in the United States
voted to add her to its liturgical calendar as a mystic and a theologian.

MORNING/EVENING PRAYER

(Psalms for Feasts, p. 75, or p. 77)

Ant 1 While I was still young, before I went on my travels, I
sought wisdom openly in my prayer.

Ant 2 I directed my soul to [wisdom], and through purification
I found her.

Ant 3 Draw near to me, you who are untaught. Why are your
souls so thirsty?

REFLECTION/SHARING

The germ of that same transcendent life, the spring of the
amazing energy which enables the great mystic to rise to
freedom and dominate [her] world, is latent in all of us; an
integral part of our humanity. Where the mystic has a genius
for the Absolute, we have each a little buried talent, some

greater, some less; and the growth of this talent, this spark of
the soul, once we permit its emergence, will conform in little,
and according to its measure, to those laws of organic growth,
those inexorable conditions of transcendence which we found
to govern the Mystic Way. Every person, then, who awakens to
consciousness of a Reality which transcends the normal world
of sense—however small, weak, imperfect that consciousness
may be—is put upon a road which follows at low levels the
path which the mystic treads at high levels.*

RESPONSORY

God is spirit and those who worship God must worship in spirit
and truth. —**God is**...
The hour is coming when the true worshipers will worship
God; —**in spirit**...
Glory to you, Source of all Being, Eternal Word and Holy Spirit.
—**God is**...

CANTICLE

Ant The connection between real holiness and homeliness is a
very close one. Sanctity comes right down to and through
all the simplicities of human life, and indeed would be of
no use to us unless it did so.**

INTERCESSIONS:

Jesus, you have invited us to drink of living waters;
—give us confidence that all are called to prayer and
contemplation.
You always did the will of the One who sent you;
—give us true detachment that leads to attachment to
God's purposes.
You have revealed to the mystics the secrets of your heart;
—may we know them as friends and guides for our journey.

Your Church is experiencing the universal call to holiness;
   —give wisdom and insight to those who serve in all forms of
      spiritual leadership.
Evelyn struggled for spiritual and intellectual integration;
   —may she inspire those who have the same struggle today.
Evelyn saw deeply into the mystery of God in the daily and the
ordinary;
   —open our eyes to all the Incarnation means.

PRAYER: O God, we pray in awe at the realization of your
presence to us. Give us the grace to be present to
you. Help us to open our minds to your guidance
and our hearts to your creative love, allowing our
very being to reveal you to the world. We ask this
through Jesus who has shown us the Way. Amen.

* Excerpt from *Mysticism* © 1911 by Evelyn Underhill, Methuen & Co., Ltd.,
London.
** Excerpt from *The Ways of the Spirit* by Evelyn Underhill.

July 2
ELIZABETH LANGE

Elizabeth Lange, a Cuban refugee born into a racially mixed marriage,
organized a free school for black children in her home (about 1827).
Eventually she founded the Oblate Sisters of Providence, the first
congregation for women of color, and pronounced her vows on July 2, 1829.*

MORNING/EVENING PRAYER

(Psalms for Feasts, p. 75; Social Justice, p. 82)

Ant 1 Open to me the gates of justice, that I may enter and
give thanks.

Ant 2 God is a stronghold for the oppressed, a stronghold in
times of trouble.

Ant 3 Open your mouth, judge righteously, maintain the
rights of the poor and needy.

REFLECTION/SHARING

I consider that the sufferings of this present time are not worth comparing with the glory that is to be revealed to us. For the creation waits with eager longing for the revealing of the children of God; because creation itself will be set free from its bondage to decay and obtain the glorious liberty of the children of God. (Rom 8:18–23)

RESPONSORY

I sent you out with sorrow and weeping, but God will bring you back with joy and gladness. —**I sent...**
Your children were taken away like a flock carried off by the enemy. —**but God...**
Glory to you, Source of all Being, Eternal Word and Holy Spirit. —**I sent...**

CANTICLE

Ant Whoever receives one such child in my name receives me; and whoever receives me, receives not me but the One who sent me.

INTERCESSIONS:

O God, your daughter, Elizabeth, founded the first religious community for women of color;
   —may her courage in the midst of great opposition inspire other women of color who must endure ridicule and rejection.
Insulted by white Catholics as well as by those who opposed Catholicism, Elizabeth continued to teach children of color;
   —forgive our prejudice and narrow-mindedness.
During the cholera epidemic of 1832, all eleven members of her community cared for patients in Baltimore's almshouse;
   —bless all those who risk their own well-being to serve those with contagious diseases.
Lacking diocesan support and experiencing prejudice from some members of the clergy, Elizabeth took in washing to keep her school going;
   —strengthen all women who are denied the support of those in authority.

During Elizabeth's lifetime, the black Oblates were denied Catholic college education;
—may the sins of the past sharpen our awareness of present-day discrimination toward people of other races, cultures, and nationalities.

PRAYER: O God, we praise you for the life and work of our sister, Elizabeth, and we ask your forgiveness for too long ignoring the accomplishments of women of different races and nationalities. Open our eyes to see the contributions of others who serve you and our world. Make us mindful of the good that is done and the grace to acknowledge it so that they may know our encouragement and support. We ask this in the name of Jesus. Amen.

* Material taken from *Women in Church History* © 1990 by Joanne Turpin, St. Anthony Messenger Press, Cincinnati.

July 14
BLESSED KATERI TEKAWITHA

It is believed that Kateri Tekawitha was born ca. 1656. Kateri was of the Indian Nation of the Iroquois (Mohawks). Born of a Christian mother (an Algonquin) who had a very good influence on her, Kateri remained faithful to her mother's teachings even after her mother's death. She endured many trials and afflictions in being faithful to the following of Christ, and died April 17, 1680.

MORNING/EVENING PRAYER
(Psalms for Feasts, p. 75; Creation, p. 59)

Ant 1 From the mouths of the innocent you have perfected praise.

Ant 2 You have come to your people to set them free.

Ant 3 Earth's peoples and all living creatures sing your praise.

REFLECTION/SHARING

May all things move and be moved in me
   and know and be known in me
May all creation
   dance for joy within me.

Chinook Psalter

RESPONSORY

Ho! All ye of the heavens, all ye of the air, all ye of the earth:
   I bid you all to hear me! —**Ho! All ye**...
Into your midst has come a new life! —**I bid**...
Glory to you, Source of all Being, Eternal Word and Holy Spirit.
   —**Ho! All ye**...

CANTICLE

Ant May our bodies, our minds, our spirits learn a new
     rhythm paced by the rhythmic pulse of the whole created
     order.

INTERCESSIONS:

Bless the wisdom of the Holy One above us; bless the truth of
the Holy One beneath us:
    Bless the love of the Holy One within us.

God of the universe, you created the land, the seas, and the
heavens;
   —give us the wisdom to respect and care for our natural
     resources as do our native peoples.
God of the living, you created the birds, the fish, and all the
animals;
   —enable us to protect their environment and to preserve the
     rights of every species that share our planet with us.
God of the holy, you reveal yourself in every time and age;
   —we give you thanks for all primitive peoples who recognized
     the holy in beasts, rocks, plants, and all the elements of
     our earth.

God of our ancestors, you revealed yourself through dreamers, seers, and prophets;
   —help us to recognize and hear the prophets who speak to us today.
God of all peoples, your loving providence extends to every race and nation;
   —give us your vision and love that we may respect the rights of all peoples, especially those indigenous to our lands.

PRAYER: O God, we have sinned against you in the oppression of our native peoples. Forgive the blindness of our past and enable us to atone for our guilt by restoring the rights of all people to live on their land in peace and with dignity. We ask this for the sake of all our native peoples who died because of our greed, and in the name of Jesus who brought us your forgiveness. Amen.

July 15
BLESSED ANNE-MARIE JAVOUHEY

Anne-Marie Javouhey was born in Jallanges, France, on November 11, 1779. In 1807, she founded the Sisters of St. Joseph of Cluny who dedicated themselves to the care of the sick and to teaching. Called to minister to the colonies, Anne-Marie devoted herself to the emancipation of the slaves. She died July 15, 1851.

MORNING/EVENING PRAYER

(Psalms for Feasts, p. 75, or 77)

Ant 1 What can be lacking to anyone who possesses God?*

Ant 2 God's light is given to us little by little.*

Ant 3 In bringing relief to suffering humanity, souls can be reached.*

REFLECTION/SHARING

...There is so much resourcefulness in children. It is on them that I count if God wishes to use us for such a great apostolate....*

RESPONSORY

One must try to adapt oneself to the present time so as to gain
    the world for God.* —**One must**...
Making ourselves all things to all; —**so as**...
Glory to you, Source of all Being, Eternal Word and Holy Spirit.
    —**One must**...

CANTICLE

Ant They are asking sisters everywhere to educate the girls. I
    find this is a beautiful mission. Women have such an
    influence on society.*

INTERCESSIONS:

During the French Revolution and religious persecution, Anne-Marie Javouhey at age nineteen dedicated her life to God and promised to serve children, the poor, and the sick;
    —give courage to all those who minister to others, especially
        those who endanger their lives to do so.
Anne-Marie answered the call to serve native peoples in distant lands;
    —support those who uproot themselves to serve others in
        times of trouble or in distressed areas of our world.
Distraught by witnessing slave-traffic, Anne Marie tended their suffering and worked tirelessly for the liberation of enslaved peoples;
    —free all who are still bound by our sins of prejudice,
        blindness, and indifference to the plight of others.
Falsely accused and misunderstood, Anne-Marie was deprived of the Sacraments for a period of two years;
    —comfort all who are wrongly sanctioned by ecclesiastical
        authority and give them inner peace.

Anne-Marie balanced her leadership and organizational skills
with true humility and genuine charity;
   —help us to use our gifts and talents for the service of
    others and recognize them as your gifts to us.

PRAYER: O God, we thank you for the life of Blessed Anne-
           Marie Javouhey and for the apostolic work
           continued in her followers, the Sisters of St. Joseph
           of Cluny. May they be faithful to her spirit in their
           service to the young, the poor, the sick, and the
           mentally afflicted. We ask this in the name of Jesus
           whose gospel she so faithfully followed. Amen.

* From her writings.

July 26
SAINT ANNE, GRANDMOTHER OF JESUS

MORNING/EVENING PRAYER

(Psalms for Feasts, p. 75; Mothers, p. 81)

Ant 1 The just leave an inheritance to their children's children.

Ant 2 The memory of the righteous is a blessing.

Ant 3 Wisdom has built her house and has set up her seven
     pillars.

REFLECTION/SHARING

Remember your mother and father when you sit among the
   great;
lest you be forgetful in their presence.
Rich experience is the crown of the aged,
and their boast is the fear of God. (Sir 23:14–25:6)

RESPONSORY

Your mercy, O God, is on those who fear you, throughout all
   generations. **—Your mercy**...

Most Holy be your name; —**throughout**...
Glory to you, Source of all Being, Eternal Word and Holy Spirit.
    —**Your mercy**...

CANTICLE

Ant My child, keep my words and treasure up my
    commandments; keep my commandments and live.

INTERCESSIONS:

O God, not in name only did blessed Anna "grace" her child;
    —we praise you for the blessings that come to us through
    her: Mary and Jesus.
Bless all grandparents, living and dead;
    —may their goodness and wisdom continue to inspire and
    encourage us.
Bless our children with the gift of time with their grandparents;
    —let them hear their history, the joys and sorrows of those
    who have given life to them.
Grant to those who have no grandchildren the blessing of Saint
Anne;
    —that they may "grandparent" the children of their
    neighborhoods and those who need their love.
Be merciful to all who must bear the breakup of families
through violence or for whatever reason;
    —let the Mother who stood motherless at the death of her
    Son be their strength and hope.

PRAYER: O God, we rejoice in the celebration of the
        grandmother of Jesus. Let the awareness of the
        influence of others in our lives help us to realize the
        unity of all people. Deepen our desire to fulfill the
        prayer of Jesus that we all may be one. Teach us to
        revere and be nourished by the lives of those who
        have given us life. We ask this in the name of Jesus,
        faithful son and grandson, hope of the ages. Amen.

August 3
FLANNERY O'CONNOR

Flannery O'Connor was born in Savannah, Georgia, March 25, 1925. She was a gifted young writer destined for success when she discovered that she had lupus erythematosus, a deadly disease that had killed her father years earlier. She spent most of her life at her mother's farm in Milledgeville, Georgia, where she crafted some of America's great short stories and kept up a remarkable correspondence. Her stories are often about men and women who are, in her words, "Christ-haunted." Her letters and essays reveal her humor, her understanding of human nature, and the depth of her spirit. She died August 3, 1964, before her fortieth birthday.

MORNING/EVENING PRAYER

(Psalms for Feasts, p. 75, or p. 77)

Ant 1 Christ was crucified on earth and the Church is crucified in time, and the Church is crucified by all of us...because she is a Church of sinners.*

Ant 2 Faith is what you have in the absence of knowledge.*

Ant 3 Mystery isn't something that is gradually evaporating. It grows along with knowledge.*

REFLECTION: Equinox [the donkey] is expecting the Humpty Dumpty Kindergarten Tuesday morning at nine-thirty. Every year we have the nursery school and the first grade and the various kindergartens.... The children go all over the yard and see the ponies and the peacocks and the swan and the geese and the ducks and then they come by my window and I stick my head out and the teacher says, "And this is Miss Flannery. Miss Flannery is an author." So they go home having seen a peacock and a donkey and a duck and a goose and an author....*

RESPONSORY

Remember that charity is beyond reason, and that God can be known through charity.* —**Remember**...
We know that God is love, —**and that**...
Glory to you, Source of all Being, Eternal Word and Holy Spirit.
   —**Remember**...

CANTICLE

Ant Learn what you can, but cultivate Christian skepticism. It will keep you free—not free to do anything you please, but free to be formed by something larger than your own intellect or the intellects of those around you.*

INTERCESSIONS:

The people I write about certainly don't disgust me entirely though I see them from a standard of judgment from which they fall short;*
  —forgive us for the times we have "put down" or "discounted" others as persons of "lesser" value.
We are not judged by what we are basically. We are judged by how hard we use what we have been given;*
  —grant that we may know our talents and use them to bring our world to a better quality of life.
Success means nothing to God, nor gracefulness. This person tries and tries violently and has a great deal to struggle against and overcome;*
  —help us to be nonjudgmental toward others.
Human nature is so faulty that it can resist any amount of grace and most of the time it does;*
  —fill us with gratitude for your mercy and unconditional love.
It is what is invisible that God sees and that the Christian must look for;*
  —give us a loving spirit that we may see with the eyes of the heart.

PRAYER: O God, we thank you for the creative gifts of writers who challenge us to see the profound in the simple and bizarre; to see your presence in the unloving and unloved. We thank you for the deep faith of Flannery O'Connor, for her humor, and for her gracious acceptance of the lupus that led to her early death. As her gifts have enriched us, so may we use our gifts to enrich others. We ask this in the name of Jesus. Amen.

* Excepts taken from *Letters of Flannery O'Connor: The Habit of Being* © 1980 by Farrar Straus & Giroux, New York.

August 8
BLESSED MARY MacKILLOP*

Mary MacKillop, born of Scottish parents in Melbourne in 1842, founded with Rev. Julian Tenison Woods the Congregation of the Sisters of St. Joseph of the Sacred Heart. Their vision brought to life a new and radical form of religious life that took the sisters in small groups to live in primitive dwellings among the pioneering people of the Australian bush. A woman before her time, she was forthright, assertive, loving, simple, and intensely loyal to the Church, even when excommunicated and removed from the leadership of her Congregation. Mary committed her life to the poor and destitute, establishing orphanages, refuges for women and children, and schools for the poor and isolated children. Mary died in 1909 and was beatified January 19, 1995.

MORNING/EVENING PRAYER

(Psalms for Feasts, p. 75, or p. 77)

Ant 1 Out of your infinite glory, O Christ, you give us the power through your Spirit for our hidden selves to grow strong.

Ant 2 It is those who are poor according to the world that God chooses to be rich in grace.

Ant 3 I believe that nothing can happen that will outweigh the supreme advantage of knowing Christ Jesus, my Lord.

REFLECTION/SHARING

To me, the will of God is a dear book which I am never tired of reading, which has always some new charm for me.**

Be kind to each other, bear with one another, bear with the faulty as you hope God will bear with you. God loves us all, but [God] loves those best who help the weak to become more perfect.**

My heart sinks almost at some things, or rather it would sink but for the firm conviction that God's words can never fail, and that God is stronger than the world which opposes [God's] teachings so much in the present day.**

In praying with the will let us not seek to make fine speeches to God, but simple affectionate appeals—if possible entirely from the heart.**

Poor houses, poor garments, etc., are all exterior show if there is not a true spirit of poverty in our hearts. It is not always the poorest dressed and the poorest housed who are the poorest before the searching eyes of God.**

RESPONSORY

It is I, your God, who teach you what is good for you. —It is...
I lead you in the way you must go, —and teach...
Glory to you, Source of all Being, Eternal Word and Holy Spirit.
　—It is...

CANTICLE

Ant As for me, the only thing I can boast about is the cross of our Lord Jesus Christ.

INTERCESSIONS:

Most holy and loving God, your Incarnate Word, Jesus Christ, was the source and inspiration of Mary MacKillop's life. In gratitude, we pray:
　　We praise you, we bless you, we glorify you.

With great trust in your providence, Mary MacKillop was open and ready to meet the needs of her time;
　—grant that we may meet the challenges of today's world
　　with faith and courage.
Mary suffered misunderstanding, calumny, and wrongful excommunication with peace and humility;
　—may we also bear with peace and humility any difficulties
　　we meet in your service.
Mary had a deep love of your will and a readiness to embrace the cross;
　—grant us the courage to follow her in accepting all that is
　　painful in our lives.
Mary MacKillop spent her life caring for the poor and destitute and educating the children of the poor;
　—grant that we may bring love and compassion to all whom
　　we serve.

PRAYER: God of mercy and compassion, you called Blessed Mary MacKillop to be the foundress of a religious congregation committed to the education of poor children and to the service of those in need. We thank you for all who have followed in her footsteps and for the love and concern shown to others through them. We ask you to bless them and those they serve in the name of Jesus who is our Way, our Truth, and our Life. Amen.

* Composed by the Sisters of St. Joseph, Australia.
** Excerpts taken from her writings.

August 9
BLESSED EDITH STEIN

Edith Stein, born into a Jewish family, October 12, 1891, was a brilliant philosopher, teacher, and a Carmelite Nun, who lost her life in an Auschwitz death camp on August 9, 1942.

MORNING/EVENING PRAYER

(Psalms from Feasts, p. 75; Social Justice, p. 82)

Ant 1 God is truth, and whoever seeks the truth is seeking God, whether [they] know it or not.*

Ant 2 "Follow me." We too are confronted with these words, and the decision they pose between light and darkness.*

Ant 3 I am convinced that whenever God calls someone, it is not for the sake of that person alone.*

REFLECTION/SHARING

Hear my prayer, O God;
let my prayer come to you!
For my days pass away like smoke,
   and my bones burn like a furnace.
My heart is smitten like grass, and withered;
   I forget to eat my bread.
Because of my loud groaning
   my bones cleave to my flesh.

All the day my enemies taunt me,
   those who deride me use my name for a curse.
For I eat ashes like bread,
   and mingle tears with my drink,
because of your indignation and anger;
   for you have taken me up and thrown me away.
My days are like an evening shadow;
   I wither away like grass. (Ps 102:1, 3–5, 8–11)

RESPONSORY

Where you go, I will go; where you die, I will die. —**Where**...
Your people shall be my people; —**where you die**...
Glory to you, Source of all Being, Eternal Word and Holy Spirit.
   —**Where**...

CANTICLE

Ant Far be it from me to glory except in the cross of our Lord
   Jesus Christ, by which the world has been crucified to me,
   and I to the world.

INTERCESSIONS:

O God, the Holocaust, the crucifixion of a people, still wounds
our hearts;
   —we beg for the grace to banish such evil from the world.
For the Christian there is no such thing as a "stranger." There
is only the neighbor—the person most in need of our help;*
   —God our Creator, help us to see that we are one human
      family.
The mystic is simply a person who has experiential knowledge
that God dwells in the soul;*
   —Spirit of God, help us to remember that we are your
      temple.
I joyfully accept in advance the death God has appointed for
me.*
   —O God, give us an acceptance of your will that perseveres
      to the end.

Come, Rosa. We are going for our people.*
—Jesus, grant us the love and courage to die for one
another.

PRAYER: O God, through her love for truth, you led Blessed
Edith Stein to the very core of Divine Wisdom. Her
life of prayer and simplicity prepared her for the
martyrdom that would bear witness to her complete
acceptance of the mystery of faith. An angel of
mercy to those imprisoned with her, she was light
and love in the midst of the darkness of evil. Let the
message of her life and the death of all victims of
the Holocaust open us to your call to transformation
of ourselves and of our world. We ask this in Jesus'
name. Amen.

* Excepts taken from *Edith Stein, A Biography* © 1985 by Harper & Row, New
York.

August 11
ST. CLARE OF ASSISI

Clare was born in Assisi in 1193. Inspired by the preaching of Francis, she
desired to live the life of holy poverty. She founded the order of Poor Clares
who lived an austere life performing many works of charity. Her spirituality
was totally formed by her love of poverty. She was known for her gift of
healing, her kindness to her Sisters, and her love of the Eucharist.

MORNING/EVENING PRAYER

(Psalms for Feasts, p. 75, or p. 77)

Ant 1 The realm of heaven is promised and given by the Lord
Jesus only to the poor: for those who love temporal
things lose the fruit of love.*

Ant 2 O blessed poverty, who bestows eternal riches on those
who love and embrace her!*

Ant 3 Place your mind before the mirror of eternity! Place your
soul in the brilliance of glory!*

REFLECTION/SHARING

...on bended knees and bowing low with both [body and soul], I commend all my sisters, both those present and those to come,...that out of the love of the God who was placed poor in the crib, lived poor in the world, and remained naked on the cross, [our Protector] may always see to it that this little flock which the [good God] has begotten in [our] holy Church by the word and example of our blessed father Francis by following the poverty and humility of [Christ Jesus] and...[the] glorious Virgin Mother, observe the holy poverty that we have promised to God....*

RESPONSORY

Look to heaven that invites us, O dearly beloved, and take up
    the cross.* —**Look to**...
Follow Christ who goes before us; —**and take**...
Glory to you, Source of all Being, Eternal Word and Holy Spirit.
    —**Look to**...

CANTICLE

Ant Place your heart in the figure of the divine substance, and
        transform your entire being into the image of the Godhead
        through contemplation.*

INTERCESSIONS:

O God, your daughter Clare courageously left all to follow the
gospel and became the foundress of a new order;
    —bless all who follow the Franciscan way of life in their
      efforts to live the gospel as Francis and Clare enjoined
      them.
Holy poverty was Clare's treasure and delight;
    —teach us simplicity in this consumer society and help us
      to trust in your loving providence.
It was through poverty that Clare was able to be a woman of
prayer;
    —keep our hearts free from clutter so that they may be
      centered on you.

Clare wanted her sisters to grow in the likeness of Christ and to be witnesses of sisterly charity;
  —help us to proclaim the gospel by our loving relationships with one another.
Though she lived in an enclosed community, Clare's light continues to shed its rays throughout the world;
  —send your healing love to those who suffer wherever they may be.
Through the holy friendship Francis shared with Clare;
  —grant that our deep friendships may show us the radiant face of Christ ever more clearly.

PRAYER: O God, through the preaching of Francis, your daughter Clare, a woman of noble birth, embraced a life of total poverty. Trusting solely on the generosity of others and holy providence, she and her followers found happiness in austerity. Bless all throughout the world who have embraced her spirit. May they continue to be a sign of your loving care and may all who follow your gospel know the gift of true simplicity and poverty of mind and heart. We ask this in the name of the poor Christ who first showed us the way. Amen.

* Excerpts from her writings.

August 15
ASSUMPTION OF MARY

MORNING/EVENING PRAYER
(Psalms for Feasts of Our Lady, p. 79)

Ant 1 A great sign appeared in heaven; a woman clothed with the sun.

Ant 2 Rejoice, O Heaven, and you that dwell therein.

Ant 3 Thanks be to God, who gives us the victory over death through Jesus Christ, alleluia.

REFLECTION/SHARING

I John am he who heard and saw these things. "Behold, I am coming soon, bringing my recompense to repay every one for what they have done. I am the Alpha and the Omega, the first and the last, the beginning and the end."..."I Jesus have sent my angel to you with this testimony for the churches. I am the root and the offspring of David, the bright morning star." (Rev 22:8–12, 13)

RESPONSORY

Blessed are you, O Mary, for your faith in the word of God.
   —Blessed...
The Most High exalts you forever; **—for your**...
Glory to you, Source of all Being, Eternal Word and Holy Spirit.
   —Blessed...

CANTICLE

Ant   God is glorified in Mary, who is taken into heaven and intercedes for us in her loving kindness.

INTERCESSIONS:

O God, you are blessed in your angels and saints. Most blessed are you in your daughter, Mary. In joy we proclaim:
             You have lifted up the lowly.

You called Mary to be the new Eve, the gate of heaven;
   —as we ponder your word, enkindle our hearts with love for your will.
Through the intercession of Mary;
   —number us among your saints in glory.
Mary's glory is her union with your will;
   —through her intercession may we always do what is pleasing to you.
Jesus, your mother was your first disciple;
   —as we meditate on the words of your gospel, may they bear fruit in our lives.

PRAYER: Glory to you, O God, in the entrance to eternal life of the ever Blessed Virgin Mary. Through her intercession, may we live the gospel of Jesus with constancy and love. As we celebrate her joy, may we imitate her fidelity. We ask this in the name of Jesus, the Eternal Word, who lives with you and with the Holy Spirit forever. Amen.

August 18
ST. JANE FRANCES DE CHANTAL

Jane Frances was born in Dijon, France, in 1572. She was married and mother of four children (two others having died as newborns) when her husband was killed in a hunting accident. After years of widowhood that included care of the sick and poor, she founded the Visitation Order in collaboration with St. Francis de Sales. She was a wise and gentle administrator of her Order and spiritual director to women and men. Jane Frances died December 13, 1641. Her surviving children were three daughters and one son.

MORNING/EVENING PRAYER

(Psalms for Feasts, p. 75, or p. 77)

Ant 1 I learned what I had never before truly understood, that one must not seek all one's consolations in creatures but in God and that the true means of being healed consists in relying upon and abandoning oneself to the divine mercy without any reservation.*

Ant 2 I felt such indescribable longings to know and follow the will of God, whatever might happen.*

Ant 3 Those who are in the world need [particular friendships] in order to secure and assist one another amid the many dangerous passages through which they must pass.*

REFLECTION/SHARING

Do not concern yourselves with your pains or confusion, nor with the dismay or terror that this may cause you although they feel violent or frightening. Instead, look to God patiently and let it be....

My solace is to have none at all; my death is not to die; my wealth is the poverty and nakedness of the cross where my Savior died stripped of the consolation of both heaven and earth: this is my path, I do not wish any other.*

RESPONSORY

My soul proclaims your greatness; my spirit has rejoiced in
  you. —**My soul**...
For your regard has blessed me; —**my spirit**...
Glory to you, Source of all Being, Eternal Word and Holy Spirit.
  —**My soul**...

CANTICLE

Ant How is it that the mother of my Lord should come to me?
  The moment I heard your greeting, the babe in my womb
  leapt for joy.

INTERCESSIONS:

We must remain in the state where God puts us: in pain, we must have patience, in suffering we must endure;*
  —grant that we may live the present moment and accept it
    as God's gift to us.
Ah, my dear sisters, our beloved Visitation is a tiny kingdom of charity;*
  —help us to live with love in our families and communities.
God has taken away from all power of any prayer...all I can do is to suffer and hold myself very simply before God...;*
  —give us the faith to believe, in times of darkness, that it is
    the Spirit who prays within us.
Never, amidst trials, lose the equanimity and peace of your heart, nor overburden it by scrutinizing your infidelities and your want of discernment;*
  —help us not to take ourselves too seriously, but trust in
    God's love and infinite mercy.

A widow, a mother, a God-seeker, foundress of the Visitation
Order, Jane Frances de Chantal followed the urgings of her
heart to be all for God;
> —help us to accept the circumstances of our life as an
> invitation to deeper union with the God who lures us on
> the way to wholeness.

PRAYER: O God, under the guidance of St. Francis de Sales
you called Jane Frances de Chantal to a life of
surrender to your love and your will. We thank you
for those persons in our life who support us on our
spiritual journeys. May the Spirit of Wisdom be with
all those who companion others on their way to you,
and may all who follow the rule Jane Frances gave
her Sisters be faithful as she was faithful. We ask
this in Jesus' name. Amen.

* Excerpts taken from her letters.

August 24
SIMONE WEIL

Simone Weil, a French intellectual and student of philosophy, died of
anorexia in 1943 at the age of thirty-four. Her empathy and compassion for
the suffering of others left her outside every political party and religious
institution though she was passionately in love with God. Attached to her
grave stone is a plaque which reads: "My solitude held in its grasp the grief of
others till my death." She could be called an apostle of compassion and
ecumenism because, living as a solitary, her love encompassed the world.

MORNING/EVENING PRAYER

(Psalms for Social Justice, p. 82; Feasts, p. 75)

Ant 1 The Cross of Christ is the only source of light that is
bright enough to illumine affliction.*

Ant 2 The apparent absence of God in this world is the actual
reality of God.*

Ant 3 This world is the closed door. It is a barrier, and at the
same time it is the passage way.*

REFLECTION: Wherever there is affliction there is the Cross—
concealed, but present to anyone who chooses truth
rather than falsehood and love rather than hate.
Affliction without the Cross is hell, and God has not
placed hell upon the earth.... Monotony is only bearable
if it is lit up by the divine. But for this very reason a
monotonous life is much the more propitious for
salvation.*

RESPONSORY

Just as there is no tree like the Cross, there is no harmony
like the silence of God.* —**Just as**...
Our soul is constantly clamorous with noise;* —**there is**...
Glory to you, Source of all Being, Eternal Word and Holy Spirit.
—**Just as**...

CANTICLE

Ant If one remains constant [in affliction], what she will
discover buried deep under the sound of her own
lamentations is the pearl of the silence of God.*

INTERCESSIONS:

O God of compassion, you desire the good and happiness of all
your people. We cry out to you:
**Give bread to the poor, and ease the
burden of those in need.**

Creator of all, your love is all-inclusive;
—help us to open our hearts to every race and to the needs
of those in want.
Christ Jesus, you sent the Samaritan woman to spread the
good news;
—raise up apostles in every age that we may worship in
spirit and truth.
Christ Jesus, you lauded the faith of the Canaanite woman;
—may we recognize your Spirit that transcends our
assumptions.

Any form of consolation in affliction draws us away from love and truth;*
—may all who give themselves for others know the peace the world cannot give.

PRAYER: O God, we thank you for women like Simone Weil, who live the good news of Jesus by their lives of absolute selfless love and compassion. Teach us compassion that we too may be bearers of your gospel, that all people may know you are with us, and that all may enjoy fullness of life and someday live with you for all eternity. Amen.

* Selections from *Gateway to God* by Simone Weil © 1982, Crossroad, New York.

August 25
AMY BIEHL

Amy Biehl was born April 26, 1967, in Santa Monica, California. She was a young woman actively engaged in life around her. Amy loved music and played the flute and handbells in her church choir. She was the drum majorette for her high school band, a good swimmer, and at Stanford University, she was the captain of her diving team. Amy was also a good student, a Fulbright scholar, and spent the last year of her life in South Africa working on voter education and a study on the status of women in an emerging democracy. Two days before she was to return to the United States, where she planned to begin her doctoral studies at Rutgers, some angry young men stormed her car, smashed her windshield, beat and stabbed her to death— backlash of the apartheid system. Amy Biehl was killed August 25, 1993.

MORNING/EVENING PRAYER

(Psalms for Social Justice, p. 84 or p. 86)

Ant 1 From the womb of the morning your youth will come like dew.

Ant 2 I saw a new heaven and a new earth...coming down out of heaven from God.

Ant 3 The wedding feast of the Lamb has begun, and the bride has made herself ready.

REFLECTION/SHARING

It was Misimangu who had said, Misimangu who had no hate for any [one], I have one great fear in my heart, that one day when they turn to loving they will find we are turned to hating.

...But when the dawn will come, of our emancipation, from the fear of bondage and the bondage of fear, why, that is a secret.

Alan Paton, *Cry, the Beloved Country*

RESPONSORY

These are they who have come out of the great tribulation; they
  have washed their robes and made them white in the blood
  of the Lamb. **—These are**...
Therefore are they before the throne of God; **—they have**...
Glory to you, Source of all Being, Eternal Word and Holy Spirit.
  —These are...

CANTICLE

Ant The Most High will wipe away every tear from their eyes,
  and death shall be no more, neither shall there be
  mourning nor crying nor pain any more, for the former
  things have passed away.

INTERCESSIONS:

In August, 1992, ten nations of South Africa committed themselves to "achieve development and economic growth, alleviate poverty, enhance the standard and quality of life of the peoples of southern Africa and support the socially disadvantaged through regional integration...";
  —O God, may Amy's love and sacrifice for the people of
  South Africa help to bring this commitment to fruition.
At least 1.5 million people in South Africa have died as a direct or indirect result of regional wars;
  —help us to learn that violence cannot solve our differences
  or bring us peace.
Amy's research was on women's rights in an emerging democracy;
  —grant that the women of Africa and other developing

nations be given the opportunities for education and full
rights as citizens of their respective countries.
Amy believed in using one's gifts and talents for the greater
good of all peoples;
  —may we grow in our awareness that we are all citizens of
    one world and that each person is our sister or brother.
Amy died when she was twenty-six years old;
  —we give you thanks, O God, for the idealism and
    compassion of Amy Biehl, and for all the young women
    who work for a better world.

PRAYER: Jesus, you came that we might have life in
abundance, and for the fullness of joy, and you were
killed by those who did not know what they were
doing. Amy Biehl saw with your eyes—that we are all
one—and loved with your heart—all people as God's
children—and she, too, died forgiving those who
killed her through their own pain and ignorance.
Give us a share in her spirit, the courage and
steadfastness to face the challenge of walking your
way of love. Let her death draw us all closer together
in mutual understanding, unity, and peace. We ask
this in your name. Amen.

August 30
BLESSED JEANNE JUGAN

Jeanne Jugan founded the Little Sisters of the Poor to care for the sick , the
homeless, and the elderly. Her humility in the face of rejection by clerical
authorities was an inspiration to those who knew her and to those who
followed her. She died August 30, 1879.

MORNING/EVENING PRAYER

(Psalms for the Aging, p. 57; Feasts, p. 75)

Ant 1 The bread of the poor is the bread of God.*

Ant 2 Only the little ones are truly pleasing to God.*

Ant 3 Go and find Jesus when your patience and strength give out and you feel alone and helpless.*

REFLECTION

"...Sister Jeanne Jugan invites us to live the Gospel beatitude of poverty in the simplicity of little ones and in the joy of children of God. She invites us especially to open our heart to the elderly, so often neglected and set aside. In proclaiming this woman Blessed, the Church intends to emphasize the charism of service rendered to the aged and, in this way, to manifest honor and love to all people advanced in age, to whom such due tribute of honor and love is sometimes denied."

Pope John Paul II

RESPONSORY

May Christ dwell in your hearts through faith; and charity
   be the root and foundation of your life. —**May Christ**...
That you may attain to the fullness of God; —**and charity**...
Glory to you, Source of all Being, Eternal Word and Holy Spirit.
   —**May Christ**...

CANTICLE

Ant It is so beautiful to be poor, to have nothing, to await all from God.*

INTERCESSIONS:

O God, you reveal your compassion for the elderly and the poor through the work of the Little Sisters of the Poor;
   —bless them as they serve those who are so special to you.
Your daughter, Jeanne, touched the hearts of all with her humility and childlike faith;
   —free us to be singlehearted; to cherish the reality that we
   are your children.
Though Jeanne Jugan founded the Order, she was unjustly overlooked and deposed as superior by ecclesiastical authority;
   —may all who suffer unjustly know God's loving compassion
   and find meaning in their trials.

Humiliated and ignored, Jeanne Jugan continued to serve the
poor and the Order with love and devotion;
   —grant that our service may always be for others and not for
   personal recognition.
Serving as a domestic for many years, the tools of her trade
were a broom, a scrubbing brush, a cleaning bucket, and a
kitchen knife;
   —may we find our self-worth in the love with which we do
   our work, rather than in prestige of position and power.

PRAYER: O Loving God, we thank you for the gift of Jeanne
Jugan to the church and to the world. In her, the
elderly and the poor, the neglected and the homeless
found an advocate and a friend. Through her
daughters, the Little Sisters of the Poor, her work
continues and your little ones are served. May all
who work to ease the suffering of the elderly be
strengthened in their task of mercy. May they know
the fullness of your peace as they follow the way of
your son, Jesus, who came to bring glad tidings to
the poor of the world. Amen.

* Excerpts from her writings.

September 17
HILDEGARD OF BINGEN

Hildegard was a twelfth-century mystic and visionary. She was a very gifted
woman: a writer, musician, healer, administrator. More insightful and
intelligent than most of those she was subject to, she gave no hint of
disrespect for legitimate authority. She was a woman of great influence
whose writings are currently gaining more attention.

MORNING/EVENING PRAYER

(Psalms for Feasts, p. 75, or p.77)

Ant 1 I prayed and understanding was given me; I called upon
God and the spirit of Wisdom came to me.

Ant 2 I preferred Wisdom to scepters and thrones, and I accounted wealth as nothing in comparison with her.

Ant 3 Wisdom I loved more than health or beauty, and I chose to have her rather than light, because her radiance never ceases.

REFLECTION/SHARING

...No creature, whether visible or invisible, lacks a spiritual life.... The clouds too have their course to run. The moon and stars flame in fire. The trees shoot forth buds because of the power in their seeds. Water has a delicacy and a lightness of motion like the wind. This is why it springs up from the Earth and pours itself into running brooks. Even the Earth has moisture and mist.*

RESPONSORY

The earth forms not only the basic raw material for humankind, but also the substance of the incarnation of God's son.*
   —The earth...
She is the mother of all that is natural, all that is human;*
   —but also...
Glory to you, Source of all Being, Eternal Word and Holy Spirit.
   —The earth...

CANTICLE

Ant Our God is the song of the angel throng and the splendor of secret ways hid from all humankind. But God our life is the life of all.*

INTERCESSIONS:

Hildegard believed that the Creator gave woman a nature deserving of respect bordering on awe;
   —may all women recognize their inherent self-worth.
She praised you, O God, in poetry and song;
   —bless all those who enrich our worship by sharing their gifts.
You gave us in Hildegard a model of a woman who theologized from the depths of her experience;
   —may our theology today reflect your interaction in our lives.

Hildegard claimed that like Mary, we too can be women
overshadowed by the Holy Spirit—vessels of the Word of God;
>   —illumine our minds and our hearts that your Word can be
>   incarnated in us.

In her visions, Hildegard saw the resurrected Christ
resplendent in feminine form;
>   —expand our images of you that we may come to know you
>   in the fullness of your being.

Through her experience with chronic illnesses, Hildegard
explored holistic ways to cure herself and others;
>   —enlighten all in the healing professions as they strive to
>   find cures and remedies for those they tend.

PRAYER: O God, we thank you for this holy woman, shy by
nature, yet fearless when she recognized your work
in her. Grant that we may recognize your work in us,
that we too may do your work on this earth—using
the gifts you have given us. Overshadow us with
your Spirit that the Word may become flesh in us
and in our world. Amen.

* Excerpts from her writings.

October 1
ST. THÉRÈSE OF LISIEUX

Mary Frances Thérèse Martin was born at Alençon in France on January 2,
1873. At the age of fifteen she obtained permission to enter the Carmelite
Monastery of Lisieux. She surrendered herself to God's merciful love,
desiring to sacrifice her life for priests and missionaries and the whole
Church. She died on September 30, 1897, at the age of twenty-four,
promising to "spend my heaven doing good on earth." She was canonized in
1925.

MORNING/EVENING PRAYER

(Psalms for Feasts, p. 75, or p. 77)

Ant 1 Love is repaid by love alone.*

Ant 2 Merit does not consist in doing or in giving much, but
rather in receiving, in loving much.*

Ant 3   Prayer is an aspiration of the heart; it is a simple glance directed to God.*

REFLECTION/SHARING

The Most High encircled her and cared for her, keeping her as the apple of her eye. Like an eagle that stirs up its nest, that flutters over its young, spreading out its wings, catching them, bearing them on its pinions, God alone did lead her.

RESPONSORY

We are the body of Christ; in the heart of the Church I will be love.* —**We are...**

I have found my vocation;* —**in the heart...**

Glory to you, Source of all Being, Eternal Word and Holy Spirit. —**We are...**

CANTICLE

Ant   God is love and they who live in love, live in God.

INTERCESSIONS:

O God, in her message, your daughter Thérèse revealed to us anew the good news that you are truly a God of gentleness and compassion;

    —may all recognize you as our Father/Mother, ever close to us.

Thérèse's life was marked by a beautiful childlike simplicity;

    —bless the children of this world; have mercy on all the abused and neglected.

She manifested a heroic trust in your loving providence;

    —give us the grace to be faithful to you and to trust in your constant care.

With childlike confidence she kept alive an ardent desire to love as she was loved;

    —we thank you for having loved us so much. Give us the grace to love one another.

Thérèse was proclaimed patroness of the missions and of gardeners;

    —help us to proclaim by our lives your boundless love and to rejoice in your beauty and your truth.

PRAYER: Merciful Mother/Father, in the simple message of Saint Thérèse is revealed anew the gospel message of love, childlike trust, and simplicity. Have mercy on all who are burdened by the complexities and unfreedoms of our daily life. Give us the grace to follow Jesus, who has set us free, in whom we live and move and have our being. Amen.

* Excerpts from her writings.

October 9
MOTHER MARY JOSEPH ROGERS, MM

Mary Josephine Rogers (Mother Mary Joseph), born in 1882, was inspired by the interest of Protestant students at Smith College for the foreign missions. Her desire to organize a group of Catholic students eventually led to founding, with Father James Walsh, the Order of Maryknoll Sisters, the first American congregation of women dedicated to the work of the foreign missions. She died October 9, 1955.

MORNING/EVENING PRAYER
(Psalms for Feasts, p. 75, or p. 77)

Ant 1 Grow so you can give.*

Ant 2 God can work miracles through your hands.*

Ant 3 Where there is love, there is no labor.*

REFLECTION:

We have tried from the beginning to cultivate a spirit which is extremely difficult and which for a long time might have been misunderstood even by those who were nearest to us, and that is, the retention of our own natural dispositions, the retention of our own individuality, having in mind, of course, that all of these things should be corrected where radically wrong, and all of it supernaturalized.... Each one of us, in her own work, with her own particular little sweetness or attractiveness, is to be used by God as a particular tool to do particular work and to save particular souls....*

RESPONSORY

Go out into the whole world, and preach the good news.
—**Go out**...
Cure the sick, heal the lepers; —**and preach**...
Glory to you, Source of all Being, Eternal Word and Holy Spirit.
—**Go out**...

CANTICLE

Ant There can be no Maryknoll Sister...who is not heroically
generous, generous to the very last inch of her
being—generous in the giving of her time, of her talents,
generous in her thoughts, generous in every possible
phase of religious life.*

INTERCESSIONS:

Witnessing the work of the Protestants for foreign missions
convinced the young Mollie Rogers (Mother Mary Joseph) that
she, too, had a work to do;
  —may our appreciation of others enable ecumenism to
    flourish, that our united efforts may build a better world.
She cautioned her Sisters to "train yourself to go up or down, in
or out, with this person or that, in any work whatsoever, and to
accept these changes readily, easily and quickly."
  —give us the humility to adapt ourselves to the situations
    of our life that are for the good of others.
Mother Mary Joseph recognized the need for professional
training for catechetical work and for evangelization;
  —bless all those who study to serve others.
Recognizing the value of contemplation, Mother Mary Joseph
established the Maryknoll Cloister to complement the work of
the Sisters in the missions;
  —help us to center ourselves so that the work that we do
    is the fruit of our relationship with you.
Mother Mary Joseph encouraged and fostered the gifts of each
of her Sisters;
  —help us to rejoice and affirm the gifts and talents of others.

PRAYER: O God, through Mother Mary Joseph Rogers, the
          first American community of women religious

missionaries was founded. Since the time of its inception, the poor, the oppressed, the sick from the far corners of the earth have known your love and concern through her followers. Through the work of Maryknoll, the blind see, the lepers are cleansed, and the poor have the Gospel preached to them. We ask your blessing on all those who continue the work of Mother Mary Joseph and pray that they may be faithful to her spirit and her vision. We ask this in your name. Amen.

* Excerpts from *Maryknoll's First Lady* © 1964 and *To the Uttermost Parts of the Earth* © 1987 by Maryknoll, New York.

October 12
CARYLL HOUSELANDER

Frances Caryll Houselander was born in Bath, England, in 1901. Although she was a writer, a poet, and an artist, above all she was a mystic with a kind of "sixth sense". She found time to work with the displaced children of Europe after the Second World War and did much work with the insane and the poor. She died October 12, 1954.

MORNING/EVENING PRAYER

(Psalms for Feasts, p. 75, or p. 77)

Ant 1 God knows our hearts and the strength of the things that assail us and the meaning of all that is incomprehensible to us.*

Ant 2 Faith is faith; it is not the realization of knowledge.*

Ant 3 Real Christianity exists in the hearts of simple people, and it depends upon one's capacity for love and for humility.*

REFLECTION/SHARING

No life is impotent before suffering, no suffering is too trifling to heal the world, too little to redeem, to be the point at which the world's healing begins.... It is true that the span of an infant's arms is absurdly short; but if they are the arms of the Divine Child, they are as wide as the reach of the arms on the Cross; they embrace and support the whole world; their shadow is the noonday shade for its suffering people; they are the spread wings under which the whole world shall find shelter and rest.*

RESPONSORY

In each comes Christ; in each, Christ comes to birth.* **—In each...**
In every cot, Mary has laid her child;* **—in each, Christ...**
Glory to you, Source of all Being, Eternal Word and Holy Spirit.
—In each...

CANTICLE

Ant I am sure that God's mercy is surrounding you.*

INTERCESSIONS:

O God, you endowed Caryll with a love for beauty from childhood;
  —open our eyes to the wonders of creation, and let it all lead us to you.
Caryll knew the "dislocating" effect of a broken home;
  —strengthen all members of broken families with all that they need to continue in love and peace.
Caryll lived the way of the cross through the ravages of war;
  —grant the grace of your sustaining Presence to all who must live through siege or armed occupation.
Prayer was the sustaining power for her through illness, doubt, and every kind of fear;
  —grant peace and aid to all who are tormented with mental or spiritual confusion.
Caryll's sensitivity to life and to suffering bore fruit in the insight and compassion that she shared in her books and poems;
  —bless all who enrich our lives by their creativity and generosity.

PRAYER: O God, the mystery of suffering and pain is a challenge to our faith. We thank you for the life and gifts of Caryll Houselander, who persevered through years of suffering, and whose reverence and love for Christ continue to be an inspiration to us. Grant us the grace to live out our lives in union with Jesus, that with him we may reveal your love and mercy to the world. This we ask in his name. Amen.

* Excepts taken from *The Letters of Caryll Houselander* © 1965 by Maisie Ward, Sheed & Ward, New York.

October 15
ST. TERESA OF AVILA

Teresa was born in Avila, Spain, in 1515. She entered the Carmelite Order, and, wishing to live the Primitive Rule, became one of its reformers. Her writings articulate the spiritual journey—from the beginning stages of prayer to the prayer of union. Because of the depth of her understanding of mystical theology, she has been named a Doctor of the Church.

MORNING/EVENING PRAYER
(Psalms for Feasts, p. 75, or p. 77)

Ant 1 There is nothing annoying that is not suffered easily by those who love one another.*

Ant 2 All must be friends, all must be loved, all must be held dear, all must be helped.*

Ant 3 Humility does not disturb or disquiet or agitate, it comes with peace, delight and calm.*

REFLECTION/SHARING

The soul understands that without the noise of words this divine Master is teaching it by suspending its faculties, for if they were to be at work they would do harm rather than bring benefit. They are enjoying without understanding how they are enjoying. The soul is being enkindled in love, and it doesn't understand how it loves. It knows that it enjoys what it loves, but it doesn't know how. It clearly understands that this joy is not a joy the intellect obtains merely through desire. The will is enkindled without understanding how. But as soon as it can understand something, it sees that this good cannot be merited or gained through the trials one can suffer on earth. This good gift is from the [One who rules] earth and heaven.... What I have described is perfect contemplation.*

RESPONSORY

Let nothing disturb you, let nothing frighten you; all things
    are passing.* —**Let nothing**...
God alone suffices;* —**all things**...
Glory to you, Source of all Being, Eternal Word and Holy Spirit.
    —**Let nothing**...

CANTICLE

Ant The important thing is not to think much but to love
    much, and so do that which best stirs you to love.*

INTERCESSIONS:

O God, you empowered Teresa to reform the Carmelite Order;
    —bless all those who seek to reform institutions; grant that
      they walk before you in sincerity and truth.
Your daughter, Teresa, had a great love for the humanity of
Jesus and cherished him as her friend;
    —may our friendship with Jesus enable us to cherish our
      friendships with one another.
Teresa taught her daughters to embrace humility, detachment,
and love for one another;
    —help us to grow in self-knowledge, to be free of hidden
      expectations, and to love those with whom we work and
      live.
You gifted Teresa with the ability to articulate the spiritual
journey and the stages of prayer;
    —through her writings, may many come to a personal
      experience of you and be consoled when the journey
      seems dark and prayer is dry.
The depth of her knowledge of the spiritual life resulted in
Teresa being proclaimed a Doctor of the Church;
    —grant that women who study theology and spirituality
      may gift the church with wisdom and insight.

PRAYER: O God, in Teresa you have given us a model—a
            woman who was faithful to prayer, to her Sisters and
            friends, and to the work she was called to do. Help
            us to be so committed to you that our daily work

fosters our life of prayer and our life of prayer enables us to live fully in the world around us—aware of its needs and concerns. Bless all who follow the charism of Teresa and grant that they may be true to her spirit and faithful to a life of prayer. We ask this through Jesus, who was ever her friend. Amen.

* Excerpts from her writings.

October 16
ST. MARGUERITE D'YOUVILLE, SGM**

Marie Marguerite Dufrost de Lajemmerais was born at Varennes, Quebec, on October 15, 1701. Through the generosity of relatives Marguerite was educated by the Ursulines in Quebec for two years. From her earliest years her life was marked by the cross. She suffered the loss of her father when she was seven; deception and humiliation by her husband, François d'Youville; and the death of four of their six children. Widowed in 1730, Marguerite managed to pay off her husband's considerable debts and to educate her two sons, who later became priests. A pioneering woman of deep faith, ever conscious of Divine Providence, she devoted herself to the care of the most destitute. This is the woman chosen by God to found the Sisters of Charity of Montreal, "Grey Nuns," in 1737 and to direct it until her death in 1771. Her work continues through her spiritual children who form six autonomous Grey Nun congregations. In perpetuating her charism throughout the world, they bear witness to the compassionate love of God in multiple works of charity.

MORNING/EVENING PRAYER
(Psalms for Feasts, p. 75, or p. 77)

Ant 1 Providence is wonderful; it has incomprehensible motives; it provides for everything. In it is all my trust.*

Ant 2 Is there any joy in life greater than that of a happy home? All the goods of earth cannot approach it.*

Ant 3 Crosses there must be, but love makes us strong enough to bear them.*

REFLECTION/SHARING

Always be faithful to the duties of the way of life you have chosen.... But above all, behave in such a way that the most perfect union will reign among you.*

RESPONSORY

She reaches out her hands to the poor and extends her arms
    to the needy. —**She reaches**...
The valiant woman, who can find her? —**and extends**...
Glory to you, Source of all Being, Eternal Word and Holy Spirit.
    —**She reaches**...

CANTICLE

Ant   Offer yourselves to [God] and to Jesus, and see in the poor
    the Christ whose members they have the honor to be.*

INTERCESSIONS:

Learn from the heart of [our loving God] the attitudes of love, tender concern, and compassion.*
    O God, help us to grow in this knowledge.

I leave all to Divine Providence; my confidence is in it. All that will happen is pleasing to God;*
    —provident God, may we learn to trust you completely.
Ask God to give us the strength to bear our crosses and to make a holy use of them. We need crosses in order to reach heaven;*
    —risen Jesus, strengthen us today as we follow you.
I am sincere, upright, and incapable of any subterfuge or reservation which could disguise the truth or give double meaning;*
    —Holy Spirit, give us courage as we face our adversaries.
We...consecrate ourselves, without reserve, to the service of the poor...;*
    —O God, may we recognize your presence in the poor.

It has pleased God to try us by fire...but the matter is over. You must think no more of it;*
—O God, help us to accept the difficulties in our lives, and to move on.

PRAYER: God of mercy and love, you led St. Marguerite d'Youville by the way of the cross and you willed that through her charity relief might be brought to the human miseries of her times. Grant us the courage to show compassionate love as she did, and the strength to persevere until the day when you call us to participate in the joy of all the saints. We ask this through Jesus Christ. Amen.

* Excerpts from her writings.
** Composed by the Grey Nuns of the Sacred Heart, Yardley, Pa.

October 21
JANET ERSKINE STUART

Janet Erskine Stuart, a convert to Catholicism from the Established Church of England, became Mother General of the Society of the Sacred Heart. She had the special gift of uplifting others, helping others recognize their unique gifts and use them. She insisted upon God's rights in the individual soul and the rights of the individual soul in God. She is a model for women in leadership. Mother Janet Stuart died October 21, 1914.

MORNING/EVENING PRAYER

(Psalms for Feasts, p. 75, or p. 77)

Ant 1 Love is itself an apostleship, and the condition of all apostleship, and the power of all apostleship. It makes everything possible.*

Ant 2 The real life is within; the smallest part is that which appears.*

Ant 3 How poor a life is in which there is no thirst.*

REFLECTION/SHARING

...These things that come home to us and hurt our self-love and humble us in the dust, these are some of God's best graces, full, full of promise, and never think that you are at the end of them. There will come more revelations ever more humbling, ever more intimate and ever more true. But never let them cast you down. Remember that they are birthdays, the putting away of the things of a child. And your vocation beaten by storms, will come out all the truer.*

RESPONSORY

She drew her strength from her faith; her heart was great.
  —**She drew**...
She excelled in trust in God, love of truth, and simplicity;
  —**her heart**...
Glory to you, Source of all Being, Eternal Word and Holy Spirit.
  —**She drew**...

CANTICLE

Ant Remember that whatever happens, "This is part of the story," and the story is God's love for you and yours for [God].*

INTERCESSIONS:

I live in confidence because I have nothing else to live in;*
  —O God, let our trust in you bear witness to your constant care and fidelity.
One real laborer is worth ten mediocrities;*
  —Jesus, make us aware of our talents and give us the courage and generosity to employ them in the spirit of the gospel.
Look if you wish to reap a harvest, but look thoughtfully, patiently, watchfully, and know why you look;*
  —wisdom of God be with us as we labor to discern call and direction in our lives.
We love the earth because it is a parable of heaven;*
  —God our Creator, open our minds and hearts to the mystery of your Being and your will.

My head is full of plans and dreams of what might be done, but
I must be patient: people are not ready yet;*
  —let our concern for others temper our zeal, and enable
  those who lead to bring us to truth and wholeness of life.

PRAYER: O God, Janet Stuart combined great desires with
deep humility, serving you with heroic hope. As
leader, she inspired others to love the best and
noblest, trusting in your grace for fruition in their
lives. Grant us renewed zeal in our daily efforts to
dedicate ourselves to you wholeheartedly. Let our
perfection consist in total openness to your will and
unfailing confidence in your love. We ask this in
Jesus' name. Amen.

* Excepts taken from *Life and Letters of Janet Erskine Stuart* by Maud
  Monahan, 1922, Longmans, Green and Co., London.

October 23
FIVE ADORERS OF THE BLOOD OF CHRIST
MISSIONARIES IN LIBERIA*

Mary Joel Kolmer, Shirley Kolmer, Kathleen McGuire, Agnes Mueller, and
Barbara Ann Muttra were American Sisters of the Adorers of the Blood of
Christ, province of Ruma, Illinois. They served the poor, the sick, and the
powerless of Liberia, West Africa, a country ravaged by civil war. Their
faithfulness to their people brought them to their deaths: two of them on
October 20, 1992, while traveling to help a sick child, the other three, shot
by soldiers at the convent gate on October 23, 1992. Their lives and deaths
bear witness to Christ's redeeming love, which gives meaning to human
suffering and death.

MORNING/EVENING PRAYER

(Psalms for Social Justice, p. 82; Feasts, p. 75)

Ant 1 In the breaking of their bodies, they seem to transcend
the limits of place and time and become teachers to the
world.

Ant 2 Let us become an evermore credible witness of God's tender love, of which the blood of Jesus is vibrant sign and unending covenant pledge.

Ant 3 They have survived the period of trial and have been deemed worthy to be numbered among the martyrs who have given their lives and shed their blood so that others may know life and freedom.

REFLECTION/SHARING

I'm glad that I came. There have been learnings in pain, vulnerability and suffering, which I probably would not have allowed myself to experience in another place and culture.

Sister Agnes Mueller

...What these five women are telling us today is simply this— you, too, have a holy mission that comes out of your baptism; that is, out of your intimate relationship with the Spirit of Jesus who leads you where it seems to fit. Indeed if we had the eyes of faith we might have seen, might have understood, what John finally recognized; namely, that the descent of the Holy Spirit makes each one of us very special and will lead you as [the Holy Spirit] led them to mission here and there and anywhere the Spirit chooses to send you, in order that you might bring the love of God to bear on those most distant and difficult places in your own world.

Archbishop James Keleher

RESPONSORY

They lived the liberation of the blood of Christ and died in love's
   service. —**They**...
They sought to be ministers of reconciliation; —**and died**...
Glory to you, Source of all Being, Eternal Word and Holy Spirit.
   —**They**...

CANTICLE

Ant In memory of Jesus and by the power of his blood, we choose to love our enemy and pray for those who have persecuted our body and our blood.

INTERCESSIONS:

Blood of Christ, courage of martyrs:
> **Bring us to life.**

For leaders of our world and our Church;
> —may they have the courage to be people of vision like
> Sister Shirley.

For those in anxiety or despair;
> —may they be touched by the kind of joy that characterized
> Sister Mary Joel.

For people in war-torn nations;
> —may the justice and peace that Sister Kathleen so
> desired come to them.

For women throughout the world;
> —may their personal dignity be affirmed through the
> perseverance of others like Sister Agnes.

For the sick, the homeless, and the oppressed;
> —may they experience care and concern ministered by
> persons with the commitment of Sister Barbara Ann.

PRAYER: O great and freeing Spirit, fill us as we journey on, walking in hope, for death has never won. The five Adorers of the Blood of Christ, missionaries in Liberia, walked the way before us in gospel love. They are our strength; we, their hope. They are our seed; we, their fruit. They are our past; we, their future. Their lives now join the martyred of your land and we join with the dreamers of the dream. O deep and stirring Spirit, come be with your people, who, through suffering, turn dreaming toward the dawn. Amen.

* Compiled by the Adorers of the Blood of Christ, Ruma, Illinois.

November 4
RAISSA MARITAIN

Raissa Maritain was a philosopher and author. After her death, her husband, Jacques Maritain, found her journals, which revealed the depth of her spiritual life. Though vitally interested in the world of her time, her spiritual path closely parallels that of St. Thérèse of Lisieux. She was a contemplative living in the everyday world. Raissa died November 4, 1960.

MORNING/EVENING PRAYER

(Psalms for Feasts, p. 75, or p. 77)

Ant 1 There is only one perfect gratuitous act—creative and saving Love.*

Ant 2 In the face of war: "Let poetry do penance, let her be silent, because she has not words for the reality of our time."*

Ant 3 A Catholic must first rediscover...the profound liberty of the children of God and that this liberty harmonizes with the whole of truth.*

REFLECTION/SHARING

We walk in darkness, risking bruising ourselves against a thousand obstacles. But we know that "God is Love," and trust in God is our light. I have the feeling that what is asked of us is to live in the whirlwind, without keeping back any of our substance, without keeping back anything for ourselves, neither rest nor friendships nor health nor leisure—to pray incessantly and that even without leisure—in fact to let ourselves pitch and toss in the waves of the divine will till the day when it will say: "That's enough."*

RESPONSORY

Our happiness is not innocent. Our joy is taken on the Cross.
  —**Our happiness**...
On our innocence there are stains of blood; —**Our joy**...
Glory to you, Source of all Being, Eternal Word and Holy Spirit.
  —**Our happiness**...

CANTICLE

Ant We breathe in God, down into the deepest and most silent recess of the soul, and the breath we breathe out with our lips can be a word and song of love.*

INTERCESSIONS:

O God, with gifts of deep and uncommon wisdom, Raissa shared her knowledge and experience of you with the world;
—grant philosophers and theologians the insights they need to magnify your name and to reveal the truth of your love to all.
Raissa had a deep compassion for all in search of love and truth;
—open our minds and hearts to the ways that you reveal yourself to us each day.
"Fear nothing" was Raissa's prayerful response to her deep longing to lead others to know and love you;
—help us to realize the treasure of the gospel, and inspire us with zeal to share it with others.
Raissa prayed for the desire to shed her blood for her faith in you;
—give the grace of courage and perseverance to all who face martyrdom today.
Raissa retained the gift of simplicity while inspiring some of the great minds of her time;
—bless all of us with a singlehearted desire to serve you and one another.

PRAYER: God of wisdom, you have revealed the beauty of truth and the tenderness of love through the life and writing of Raissa Maritain. She persevered in faith through the challenges of philosophy and through the terror of war. May all philosophers be as deeply and simply dedicated to truth, and may all Christians be inspired by her goodness. We ask this in Jesus' name. Amen.

* Excepts taken from *Raissa's Journal* © 1974 by Magi Book Inc., Albany.

November 11
CATHERINE McAULEY

Catherine McAuley, a well-educated woman, spent most of her adult life helping the poor in the city of Dublin. At the age of forty, she dedicated herself entirely to serving the poor. She founded the Order of Sisters of Mercy in 1831 and died ten years later, November 11, 1841.

MORNING/EVENING PRAYER

(Psalms for Feasts, p. 75, or p. 77)

Ant 1 Blessed are the merciful for they shall obtain mercy.

Ant 2 Teach me goodness, discipline and knowledge.*

Ant 3 However painful the cross may be which you have prepared for me, I await it through your grace with entire submission.*

REFLECTION/SHARING

...We have one solid comfort amidst this little tripping about, our hearts can always be in the same place, centered in God, for whom alone we go forward or stay back. Oh may [God] look on us with love and pity and then we shall be able to do anything [God] wishes us to do, no matter how difficult to accomplish or painful to our feelings.*

RESPONSORY

I desire only to do your will, my God.* —**I desire**...
To serve you in your people,* —**and to do**...
Glory to you, Source of all Being, Eternal Word and Holy Spirit.
   —**I desire**...

CANTICLE

Ant Whatever you do to the least of my people, you do to me.

INTERCESSIONS:

O God, you chose Catherine McAuley to found an order dedicated to works of mercy. With grateful hearts we pray:
   We praise you; we thank you; we glorify you.

Reared in a family with different religious persuasions,
Catherine experienced love and returned love;
   —grant that the differences among us may enable us to grow
     in respect and appreciation for one another.
You call us to mercy rather than to sacrifice;
   —give us a spirit of moderation in all that we do.
Like Mary beneath the cross, Catherine suffered the loss of
many she dearly loved;
   —strengthen those who attend and serve loved ones who are
     dying.
In your wisdom you led Catherine to found the Sisters of
Mercy;
   —grant them the graces they need to carry on your work in
     this world.

PRAYER: O God, the poor and needy are with us always.
Through the intercession of Catherine McAuley,
help us to recognize them in our families, our
communities, as well as in our cities, and in places
far away. May they know your care and concern in
those who minister to them. This we ask of you
through the mercy of Jesus, who died that we may
live. Amen.

* Excerpts from her writings.

November 13
ST. FRANCES XAVIER CABRINI

Frances Xavier Cabrini founded the Missionary Sisters of the Sacred Heart
in Codogno, Italy. She came to the United States in 1889 and eventually
became a citizen. She established schools, hospitals, and orphanages. She
died in Chicago on December 22, 1917, and became the first citizen of the
United States to be canonized.

MORNING/EVENING PRAYER
(Psalms for Feasts, p. 75, or p. 77)

Ant 1 How blessed the woman whose heart goes out to the
poor; those who trust in God delight in showing mercy.

Ant 2 Go out to all nations and spread the word of the gospel.

Ant 3 You are the light of the world; a city set on a hill cannot be hidden.

REFLECTION/SHARING

The Spirit of God is upon me,
    because God has anointed me
to bring good tidings to the afflicted;
sending me to bind up the brokenhearted,
    to proclaim liberty to the captives,
    and the opening of the prison to those who are bound;
to proclaim the year of God's favor,...
to grant those who mourn in Zion—
the oil of gladness instead of mourning,
the mantle of praise instead of a faint spirit. (Is 61:1, 2–3)

RESPONSORY

My heart is glad and my soul rejoices. —**My heart**...
You have shown me the path to life; —**and my**...
Glory to you, Source of all Being, Eternal Word and Holy Spirit.
    —**My heart**...

CANTICLE

Ant Jesus went about all the cities and villages, teaching in their synagogues, preaching the gospel, and healing every disease and infirmity.

INTERCESSIONS:

O Christ, you commissioned your early disciples to preach your gospel to all the nations. Throughout the centuries, women have left their native lands to spread the good news to other nations and peoples, and so we pray:
        Praise to you, Lord Jesus Christ!

Christ, our Redeemer, your Church has named Mother Cabrini the patron of emigrants;
    —may they receive welcome and hospitality in their adopted homelands.

You came to serve the lowly and the poor;
 —may the cause of justice triumph over personal and
  national greed.
As a child, you fled to Egypt for safety;
 —protect all refugees seeking asylum from unjust
  oppression.
You inspired Mother Cabrini to become a citizen of her new
land;
 —may all exercise their citizenship responsibly according to
  gospel values.
Mother Cabrini served you in the sick and poor;
 —may her work continue that they may know your love and
  your healing.

PRAYER: O God, we thank you for all the good you
accomplished through the life of Mother Cabrini, and
through those who have followed her example. May
our country be blessed with a greater desire to
embrace those seeking freedom or refuge. We ask
this through Jesus Christ who lives with you, Source
of all Being, and with the Holy Spirit, forever. Amen.

November 16
ELBA and CELINA RAMOS

Elba Julia Ramos and her daughter Celina Maricet Ramos were
murdered during the night of November 16, 1989, as they witnessed
the assassination of six Jesuit priests in El Salvador. The women had
worked as cook and housekeeper for the residence and remained
there the night of their death to be safe from curfew bombing. Elba
was thirty-nine and Celina was fifteen years old.

MORNING/EVENING PRAYER

(Psalms for Social Justice, p. 82 or p. 84)

Ant 1 God has delivered us from the power of darkness and
transferred us into the realm of God's beloved son,
Jesus.

Ant 2 We are witnesses to these things, and so is the Holy Spirit whom God has given to those who obey God.

Ant 3 As for me, in my justice I shall see your face; when I awake, I shall be filled with the sight of your glory.

REFLECTION/SHARING

There shall no more be anything accursed, but the throne of God and the Lamb shall be in it, and God's servants shall worship there; they shall see God's face, whose name shall be on their foreheads. And night shall be no more; they need no light of lamp or sun, for God will be their light, and they shall reign for ever and ever. (Rev 22:3–5)

RESPONSORY

O God, hear a cause that is just, attend to my cry. **—O God...**
If you should try my heart or visit me by night; **—attend...**
Glory to you, Source of all Being, Eternal Word and Holy Spirit.
　—O God...

CANTICLE

Ant O God, you subdue evil oppression, and challenge unjust nations. You chose our heritage for us, gave it to us out of love.

INTERCESSIONS:

O God, you hear the cry of the poor!
　—we pray that this mother and child have not died in vain.
Elba and Celina are two of the many who have died in the struggle for human rights;
　—give us the wisdom and generosity to share the world's
　goods and services.
Yours is a father's care and a mother's tenderness;
　—comfort the husband and father of these women and all
　who love them.
Human tragedy challenges our faith;
　—help us to bear and live the mystery of your ways.

Elba and Celina are our sisters, simple women like us;
—be our courage and hope at the hour of our death.

PRAYER: O God, your Holy Spirit abides in our hearts, and in you we are one. Through the suffering and death of Jesus, through the suffering and death of Elba and Celina, may we come to realize our power to support or to destroy life. Purify our minds and our hearts of all that cannot be offered for the praise of your name. Open us to your creative love that we may be sisters and brothers of the Risen Lord indeed. We ask this in Jesus' name. Amen.

November 18
ST. PHILIPPINE DUCHESNE

Philippine Duchesne was born at Grenoble, August 29, 1769. When her community of Visitation Sisters was dispersed during the French Revolution, she entered the Society of the Religious of the Sacred Heart. At the request of the bishop of Louisiana, she came to North America in 1818 and established sixteen houses of the Society for the education of youth. Toward the end of her life, she devoted herself to the service of Native Americans. Philippine Duchesne died November 18, 1852.

MORNING/EVENING PRAYER

(Psalms for Feasts, p. 75, or p. 77)

Ant 1 Come to me, all who labor and are heavy laden, and I will give you rest.

Ant 2 Go into the world, and preach the gospel to the whole creation.

Ant 3 One who loses her life for my sake will find it.

REFLECTION/SHARING

...I long for retirement and rest, and I have no hope of finding them in this life. I should not, however, want an inactivity that would expose me to the danger of napping all day long. But everything seems to point to the fact that there is no sweet retreat ahead of me. Wherever I have been, external and distracting work has been my lot and still is, though I am about to begin my seventieth year. There is still no one else here to give the morning call, make the last visit at night, care for the garden, watch by the sick, or take care of the pantry, the linen room, etc....*

RESPONSORY

Take my yoke upon you, and learn from me; for I am gentle and
　　lowly in heart. —**Take my**...
And you will find rest for your souls; —**for I**...
Glory to you, Source of all Being, Eternal Word and Holy Spirit.
　　—**Take my**...

CANTICLE

Ant　Pray always and never lose heart.

INTERCESSIONS:

O God, St. Philippine's love for the Sacred Heart of Jesus bore fruit in her dedication to the salvation of others;
　　—inspire us with ways to incarnate our love for you and to
　　　live the message of the gospel.
She left her country, family, and friends and founded houses of the Society of the Sacred Heart in America;
　　—inspire us with the generosity, detachment, and humility
　　　that marked her life.
The ladder by which she made her ascent to God was the prayer of adoration and love before the Blessed Sacrament;
　　—in times of dryness, enable us to persevere in prayer—
　　　to give you time.
The seeds of Philippine's holiness were planted in childhood;
　　—keep us faithful to the graces of the past and attentive
　　　to your spirit active in our lives now.
Philippine persevered in faith through seemingly insurmountable obstacles;
　　—give us a singlehearted dedication to you and to the
　　　mission to which we are called.

PRAYER: O God, we thank you for blessing the early years of our nation with the gift of St. Philippine Duchesne. Her heart was hollowed by detachment of every sort and opened wholly to love for you and your people everywhere. Her special care for the Native American people continued through her old age, and they knew your divine power in her life in spite of her helplessness. Bless the people of France who gave her to us, and grant us her singlehearted sense of mission. May all the world know the love of the Heart of Jesus in whose name we pray. Amen.

* Excerpts from her writings.

November 22
JEANNE FONTBONNE
(Mother St. John)

Jeanne Fontbonne was born in Basen-Basset, France, on March 3, 1759. She became a Sister of St. Joseph and served as superior of her community until she was imprisoned at the outbreak of the French Revolution. She later restored her order, sent a mission to the United States, and eventually saw the establishment of two hundred new communities. She died in Lyons on November 22, 1843.

MORNING/EVENING PRAYER

(Psalms for Feasts, p. 75, or p. 77)

Ant 1 They who sow in tears shall reap in joy.

Ant 2 All my desire is that you become saints.*

Ant 3 When I think that you are in a different world from me, I am consoled by the reflection that we are all in the bosom of our God.*

REFLECTION/SHARING

Europe does not suffice for the ardent charity of the Sisters of St. Joseph. They have undertaken to teach in foreign lands the truths of our holy religion to minds and hearts hitherto uncultivated. Those are sheep without a pastor whom you are to lead into the fold of the Church. It is a difficult task, but the Crib and the Cross have triumphed over everything.*

RESPONSORY

Love your neighbors as yourself; love them as Christ Jesus
   loves you. —**Love**...
In giving your life, —**love them**...
Glory to you, Source of all Being, Eternal Word and Holy Spirit.
   —**Love**...

CANTICLE

Ant Rely upon God who can do all things, and that most
     effectively where creatures can do nothing.*

INTERCESSIONS:

Most gracious God, we place our trust in you. In confidence we pray:

That all may be one.

O God, you raised up Jeanne Fontbonne to reorganize the Sisters of St. Joseph and to extend their services throughout the world;
   —may all missionaries be graced to walk humbly, to listen
     sensitively, and to serve justly.
You call us by name to be one with you and with one another;
   —help all teachers and ministers of your word to be living
     signs of your love.
You invite us to build our future in fidelity to your gospel message;
   —enable all members of faith communities to work for justice
     and peace, and to alleviate the causes of oppression.
You share life with us in your banquet of love;
   —may we be faithful to our commitments, respectful of our
     differences, and one in our desire to love God.

PRAYER: O God, you have shared your bountiful love and mercy with your servant Jeanne Fontbonne, and with the women inspired by her as Sisters of St. Joseph. We praise you for revealing your goodness through them, and we thank you for the gift that their commitment is to us. Grant those who serve us today the vitality, courage, and generosity to continue the work that you have begun in Jeanne Fontbonne and in them. We ask this in the name of Jesus. Amen.

* Excerpts from her writings.

November 26
SOJOURNER TRUTH

Sojourner Truth was born into slavery ca. 1790. She was freed under state law in 1827. Named Isabella, she changed her name to Sojourner Truth after a religious experience, and she became an abolitionist and a spokesperson for women's rights. She died in 1883.

MORNING/EVENING PRAYER

(Psalms for Feasts, p. 75; Social Justice, p. 82)

Ant 1 Nobody knows the trouble I've seen; nobody knows my sorrows.

Ant 2 When I cried out with my mother's grief, none but Jesus heard me!*

Ant 3 I have been forty years a slave and forty years free, and would be here forty years more to have equal rights for all.*

REFLECTION/SHARING

...The Akron convention was marked by the presence of many men of the cloth, most of whom apparently were opposed to the granting of feedom to women. One based his argument in favor of male privilege on man's greater intellect; another on the manhood of Christ; another on the sin of Eve. Finally the atmosphere of the convention became somewhat stormy. As Gage related the scene, "slowly from her seat in the corner rose Sojourner Truth."

RESPONSORY

There are no more distinctions, male or female, slave or free,
    we are one in Christ. **—There**...
Children of God, a priestly people; **—we are**...
Glory to you, Source of all Being, Eternal Word and Holy Spirit.
    —There...

CANTICLE

Ant Thou art my last master, and thy name is Truth; and
      Truth shall be my abiding name till I die.*

INTERCESSIONS:

O God, you created us all and we are equal in your sight. We cry out in hope:
> **Free at last! Free at last! Thank God Almighty,
> we're free at last!**

O God, through Moses, you led your people out of slavery;
    —raise up women and men who will free those still held in
      bondage.
O God, through Daniel, you confounded the treachery of the judges;
    —give us the courage to speak the truth and confront evil.
O God, through Esther, you saved your people from destruction;
    —bring all prejudice to light that genocide may be no more.
O God, through Sojourner Truth, you again call us to freedom;
    —open our ears and our hearts that we may hear the
      prophets of our day.

PRAYER: God of Truth and Freedom, you speak to us in every age through men and women of every race and creed, yet we fail to recognize your voice. Free us from our limitations, our prejudices and blindness that we may respect the dignity of every person on this earth. Especially today we pray for all women that they may know their freedom and use it for the good of all. We ask this in Jesus' name. Amen.

* Excerpts from her writings.

November 29
DOROTHY DAY

Dorothy Day, cofounder (with Peter Maurin) of the Catholic Worker Movement, had a passionate love for the poor, the outcast, and the downtrodden. She was a radical, a suffragist, an outspoken critic of the establishment. She was considered by many to be the most influential Roman Catholic of her time. Dorothy Day died November 29, 1980.

MORNING/EVENING PRAYER

(Psalms for Feasts, p. 75; Social Justice, p. 82)

Ant 1 When did we see you hungry and give you to eat? When did we see you thirsty and give you to drink?

Ant 2 Blessed are those who suffer persecution for the sake of justice, for God is their reward.

Ant 3 If you would be perfect, give all to the poor and come follow me.

REFLECTION/SHARING

...Certainly when I lie in jail...thinking of war and peace, and the problems of human freedom...and the apathy of great masses of people who believe that nothing can be done, I am all the more confirmed in my faith in the little way of St. Thérèse. We do the minute things that come to hand, we pray our prayers, and beg also for an increase of faith—and God will do the rest.*

RESPONSORY

She opens her heart to the poor, and reaches out her hand to the
    needy. —**She**...
She opens her mouth with wisdom; —**and reaches**...
Glory to you, Source of all Being, Eternal Word and Holy Spirit.
    —**She**...

CANTICLE

Ant God is in the midst of her, she shall not be moved.

INTERCESSIONS:

O God, you gave us Jesus to teach us that you hear the cry of
the poor and the needy. Give us hearts of flesh that we may
respond with compassion as we pray:
                    Have mercy on us!

O Christ, you reached out to the lepers and healed them;
    —help us to embrace the outcasts of our society.
You socialized with the tax collectors and sinners;
    —show us how to break down the barriers that divide us.
You talked with the Samaritan woman and healed the child of
the Canaanite woman;
    —may we learn how to cross the thresholds of prejudice.
You fed the hungry by giving them bread of wheat and the
bread of your body;
    —teach us how to feed each other.
You had compassion on the poor and the suffering,
    —may we see you in the street people, the destitute, and
      the hopeless.

PRAYER: O God, look with tender mercy on the needs of the
              poor and the alienated, and teach us to hear and
              answer their cries. We praise you for those who have
              given their lives to serve you in the poor. May they
              know your support and love as they follow the way
              of Jesus. Bless especially all who serve the poor in
              the Catholic Worker movement. We ask this in the
              name of Jesus. Amen.

* Excerpts from her writings.

November 30
ETTY HILLESUM

Etty Hillesum, born in Amsterdam, was Jewish by birth but with no religious affiliation. She was a student of psychology and literature. Journals found after her death at Auschwitz, November 30, 1943, reveal a moving story of the transformation of a woman from a fun-loving girl to a compassionate God-centered woman. She died at the age of twenty-seven.

MORNING/EVENING PRAYER

(Psalms for Social Justice, p. 84; Feasts, p. 75)

Ant 1 I shall always feel safe in God's arms.*

Ant 2 We have so much work to do on ourselves that we shouldn't even be thinking of hating our so-called enemies.*

Ant 3 I shall always labor for You and remain faithful to You, and I shall never drive You from my presence.*

REFLECTION/SHARING

...This is something people refuse to admit to themselves: at a given point you can no longer *do*, but can only *be* and accept. And although that is something I learned a long time ago, I also know that one can only accept for oneself and not for others. That is what is so desperately difficult for me here.... I have never been able to "do" anything; I can only let things take their course and if need be suffer. This is where my strength lies and it is great strength indeed. But for myself, not for others....

I see more and more that love for all our neighbors, for everyone made in God's image, must take pride of place over love for one's nearest and dearest....*

RESPONSORY

O God, you are a refuge for the oppressed, a stronghold in times of trouble. **—O God**...
Those who know your name put their trust in you;
    —a stronghold...
Glory to you, Source of all Being, Eternal Word and Holy Spirit.
    —O God...

CANTICLE

Ant Hear, O Israel: the Lord our God, the Lord is one.

INTERCESSIONS:

O God, through the life and death of Etty Hillesum, you have
given us a model of faith grown in suffering;
   —through her intercession may our openness to the Mystery
     of your love for us know no limits.
I shall never burden my today with cares about tomorrow;*
   —Spirit of God, teach us how to use our energies in creative
     ways, always trusting in your providence.
I keep finding myself in prayer. And that is something I shall
always be able to do, even in the smallest space: pray;*
   —in times of spiritual dryness, O God, help us to remember
     that your Spirit prays within us, asking for what we do not
     know how to ask.
I promise You to live as fully as I can wherever it should please
You to put me;*
   —Good Shepherd and Guide, give us the grace to persevere
     in our dedication to you when change and sorrow
     challenge our fidelity.
If I could only be there to give some of those packed thousands
just one sip of water;*
   —God, our Creator, make us anew; transform our hearts of
     stone to hearts of flesh.

PRAYER: "I often walk with a spring in my step along the
           barbed wire, and then time and again it soars
           straight from my heart—I can't help it, that's just the
           way it is, like some elementary force—the feeling
           that life is glorious and magnificent, and that one
           day we shall be building a whole new world."* God
           our Creator, God of mercy and compassion, let the
           suffering of your people bear fruit in "a whole new
           world." Amen.

* Excepts taken from *An Interrupted Life* © 1983 by Pantheon Books, New
  York.

December 2
MAURA CLARKE, MM, ITA FORD, MM,
DOROTHY KAZEL, OSU, AND JEAN DONOVAN

On the evening of December 2, 1980, two Maryknoll Sisters, Maura Clarke and Ita Ford, were returning to El Salvador from a retreat in Nicaragua. They were picked up at the airport by an Ursuline Sister, Dorothy Kazel, and a young lay woman, Jean Donovan, who worked in the refugee camps. On the road from the airport, they were stopped at a military roadblock. They were taken to a remote spot along a side road, brutally abused, and then executed. They have become part of the martyrology of the Christian communities throughout Latin America.

MORNING/EVENING PRAYER

(Psalms for Social Justice, p. 82; Feasts, p. 75)

Ant 1 Our lips will praise you, for sweeter than life is your merciful love.

Ant 2 They girded themselves with your strength. The light they have kindled will never go out.

Ant 3 Give them the reward of their deeds, for they served you in the poor.

REFLECTION/SHARING

God, in His/Her loving kindness, has raised up witnesses in our midst. God is calling each of us to a more radical discipleship—one which will not be understood by the powerful of our day. We must be wise as serpents in naming and denouncing the evil which pervades our world. We must be filled with compassion with those for whom suffering from lack of basic necessities has become a way of life. We must be moved to action which will clearly identify us with the poor. Above all, let us not be filled with fear. Let us be filled with courage and hope, for "in the tender compassion of our God, the dawn shall break upon us, to shine on those who dwell in darkness and the shadow of death, to guide our feet into the way of peace."

Sr. Melinda Roper, MM

RESPONSORY

Our God is a stronghold for the oppressed, a stronghold in
   times of trouble. —**Our**...
Those who know your name put their trust in you; —**a stronghold**..
Glory to you, Source of all Being, Eternal Word and Holy Spirit.
   —**Our God**...

CANTICLE

Ant You shall love your God with all your heart, and with all
   your soul and with all your mind, and your neighbor as
   yourself. Do this and you will live.

INTERCESSIONS:

O God, you have inspired many women to follow Jesus, your
Incarnate Word, who gave his life that we may have life. We lift
our voices and say:
> **Blessed are they who suffer persecution for
> the sake of the gospel.**

Through the witness of Maura Clarke, Ita Ford, Dorothy Kazel,
and Jean Donovan;
   —may more people be inspired to serve the homeless and the
      oppressed.
May all who have died in Latin America for the sake of justice;
   —be seeds of liberty for all the oppressed.
God of freedom, protect the poor and the helpless;
   —from the greed of large corporations and those seeking
      personal profit.
Jesus, you lived in a land held captive by imperial Rome;
   —grant all peoples the right of self-determination that they
      may forge their own destinies.
God of the Americas, Christ of the Andes, Our Lady of
Guadalupe;
   —look with love and compassion on the peoples of Central
      and South America, and grant them freedom from all
      oppression.

PRAYER: O God, Lover of the poor and oppressed, in our remembrance of these four courageous women, may we honor all the nameless women, men, and children whose lives were forfeited by violence and hatred. May they now know your peace and the joy of seeing you face to face. We ask this through the intercession of all these victims who now stand before the Lamb, singing your praises. Amen.

December 8
IMMACULATE CONCEPTION

MORNING/EVENING PRAYER

(Psalms for Feasts of Our Lady, p. 79)

Ant 1 Blessed are you, O Mary, for in you God's promise was fulfilled.

Ant 2 Mother of mercy and holy hope, be near to those who pray to you.

Ant 3 You are the new Eve, the beginning of a new creation.

REFLECTION/SHARING

Virgin most prudent
Virgin most merciful
Virgin most faithful
Seat of wisdom
Cause of our joy
Refuge of sinners
Comfort of the afflicted
Help of Christians

RESPONSORY

You have made me a vessel of salvation; a font of living water.
    —**You have...**
Within my womb springs forth, —**a font...**

Glory to you, Source of all Being, Eternal Word and Holy Spirit.
—**You have...**

CANTICLE

Ant O Mary, you are the Dawn; through you all creation will
see the Light of the World.

INTERCESSIONS:

Let us praise God who has given us Mary as a model of
holiness. We pray to her:
Mother of Christ, teach us to hear the word of God.

O Christ, be praised in Mary, comforter of the afflicted;
—teach us to be a healing presence in the lives of others.
Be praised in Mary, queen of peace;
—give us forgiving hearts and bless our world with the peace
that only you can give.
Be praised through Mary, help of Christians;
—help us all to proclaim the gospel with our lives.
Be praised in Mary, refuge of sinners;
—teach us to support one another in our efforts to follow
your will.
Be praised in Mary, ark of the covenant;
—let our lives bear witness to your abiding presence in us.

PRAYER: O God, you have given us Mary, the mother of Jesus,
to encourage and guide us on the way to union with
you. Let her life of loving obedience and humble
prayer be a beacon of light and courage for us as we
seek to follow your Christ. This we ask in the name
of that same Jesus Christ, the Eternal Word, who
lives with you and with the Holy Spirit, forever.
Amen.

December 12
OUR LADY OF GUADALUPE

MORNING/EVENING PRAYER

(Psalms for Feasts of Our Lady, p. 81)

Ant 1 I am the ever-virgin Mary, Mother of the God who gives life and maintains it.

Ant 2 I will show my compassion to your people and to all people.

Ant 3 What is troubling you, my little one? Are you not under my protection?

REFLECTION/SHARING

Lift up your eyes round about, and see;
  they all gather together, they come to you;
your sons shall come from far,
  and your daughters shall be carried in the arms.
Then you shall see and be radiant,
  your heart shall thrill and rejoice.
The glory of Lebanon shall come to you,
  the cypress, the plane, and the pine,
to beautify the place of my sanctuary. (Is 60:4, 5, 13)

RESPONSORY

Hail Mary, full of grace, the Lord is with you. —**Hail Mary**...
Blessed are you among women; —**the Lord**...
Glory to you, Source of all Being, Eternal Word and Holy Spirit.
  —**Hail Mary**...

CANTICLE

Ant From this day all generations will call me blessed.

INTERCESSIONS:

O God, through Mary, our Mother, you revealed your
compassion to the Hispanic people;
  —bless all peoples with the awareness of your tender mercy.

O God, you choose the anawim of the world to confound the mighty;
>   —give us true humility of spirit.

The image of the Mother and your Son was imprinted on the garment of Juan Diego with features of his race;
>   —imprint within us a fearless acceptance of all races and
>   peoples.

In Jesus, the Incarnate Word, you have showed us that you are ever close to us;
>   —have mercy on the downtrodden, the abused and
>   neglected of the world.

Through Juan Diego, you showed your love for the simple and the humble;
>   —forgive us for the injustices imposed on native peoples of
>   the earth and redress the wrongs they have suffered.

PRAYER: O God, of infinite compassion, you have revealed your most tender mercy in the consoling words spoken to your servant, Juan Diego, by our Lady of Guadalupe. Bless all the native peoples of the Americas and of every land and may we all come to realize that our true and lasting integrity is in Jesus, our loving Savior. Amen.

December 14
JOAN SAWYER, SSC

Joan Sawyer was born in Antrim, Ireland, on April 17, 1932. She entered the Missionary Sisters of St. Columban in Belfast. She lived in the United States for nine years, becoming a citizen and earning a degree in social work at Mundelein College. In 1977 she went to Lima, Peru, and dedicated herself to the service of the prisoners at Lurigancho Prison where she was chaplain. She became known for her fearless and delicate kindness to the prisoners and their families. On December 14, 1983, during a prison riot, she and several Sisters were taken hostage. After negotiations, the prisoners with their hostages left the prison compound where they were met with a barrage of bullets from the military. Sr. Joan and the prisoners were killed—the other hostages escaped.

MORNING/EVENING PRAYER

(Psalms for Social Justice, p. 82; Feasts, p. 75)

Ant 1 I was in prison, and you visited me.

Ant 2 The Cross pushes us to build here on earth a better world.*

Ant 3 If we are faithful to our role, what we do now will make a real difference in our world.*

REFLECTION/SHARING

Joan was inspired and enriched by [the people she served] and the way they shared the little they had. She wrote, "I am graced by their courage, their hope in spite of hardship, their joy in sharing, their faith in God, their ability to celebrate life." The day she was killed she had brought packages to two prisoners from their parents. One of them, Julio, expressed his reaction, "I can still see her eyes which reached to eternity...her spirit of kindness and sacrifice toward us prisoners will be my most precious memory." At her funeral, legal documents on which she had been working for the release of prisoners were carried in the Offertory procession.

...We pray that Joan's death might be a force to get the authorities moving to do something about the jails, the prisoners and the justice system.... Joan and her eight prisoner friends are witnesses to the unjust conditions, to the lack of respect for life....
Homily given at St. Ignatius Church (Chicago), December 16, 1984

RESPONSORY

Every person has an inherent right to live a fully human life.
—**Every person**...
Justice is essential to the healing that enables all people;
—**to live**...
Glory to you, Source of all Being, Eternal Word and Holy Spirit.
—**Every person**...

CANTICLE

Ant God has sent me to bring the Good News to the poor...to proclaim release to prisoners.

INTERCESSIONS:

O God, you have created us in your own image;
—grant that prisoners be treated with respect and dignity.
You have given us freedom and the earth as our home;
—help us in our efforts to obtain humane living conditions
in prisons that are grossly overcrowded.
Your son, Jesus, was falsely accused and imprisoned;
—may prisoners be given just legal defense, especially those
who are poor and uneducated.
Joan described life in prison saying, "I never saw so much
misery concentrated in one small area";
—relieve the hunger, sickness, and boredom experienced
by those who are incarcerated.
Jesus called those blessed who visit those in prisons;
—bless all prison chaplains and enable them to bring
comfort to those they serve.

PRAYER: O God, we give you thanks for the life of Sr. Joan
Sawyer and for her efforts to improve the lives of
prisoners. May she be an inspiration to all who work
for a just penal system and may her death obtain
the changes she courageously worked for. Enable
those who minister to prisoners recognize the face of
Jesus in the midst of degradation, corruption, and
all that is part of the prison scene. We ask this in
the name of Jesus who suffered that all may be free.
Amen.

* From her writings.

Other Inclusive Language Books Also Available

Scripture Readings: Advent to Pentecost (Vol. I)
Sundays (Cycles A, B, C) and Weekdays (Yrs. I and II);
Includes Weeks 1–9 of Ordinary Time

Scripture Readings: Ordinary Time (Vol. II)
Sundays (Cycles A, B, C) and Weekdays (Yrs. I and II);
Weeks 10–34

The New Companion to the Breviary with Seasonal Supplement:
A four-week psalter including intercessions for Ordinary
Time with propers of the seasons from Advent to
Pentecost

The New Companion to the Breviary:
A four week psalter; ideal size for traveling

Hidden Friends: Reflections from a Monastery
Prayerful reflections and art work based on writings of
Carmelite saints

INDEX OF PERSONS

CANTICLE OF ZECHARIAH

Blessed are you, God of Israel
for you have visited and redeemed your people,
and have raised up a horn of salvation for us
in the house of your servant.

As you spoke through the mouths
of your holy prophets from of old,
that we should be saved from our enemies,
and from the hand of all who oppress us;

to perform the mercy promised to our ancestors,
and to remember your holy covenant,

the oath you swore to Abraham and Sarah,
to grant us deliverance from evil,
that we might serve you without fear,
in holiness and righteousness
all the days of our lives.

And you, child,
will be called the prophet of the Most High,
for you will go before the Holy One
to prepare God's ways,

to give knowledge of salvation to God's people
in the forgiveness of their sins,

through the tender mercy of our God
when the day shall dawn upon us from on high

to give light to those who sit in darkness
and in the shadow of death,
to guide our feet
into the way of peace. Glory...